The Writing on the Wall

Everyday Phrases from the King James Bible

— RICHARD NOBLE —

Sacristy Press

Sacristy Press
PO Box 612, Durham, DH1 9HT

www.sacristy.co.uk

First published in 2014 by Sacristy Press, Durham

Copyright © Richard Noble, 2014
The moral rights of the author have been asserted

All rights reserved, no part of this publication may be reproduced or transmitted in any form or by any means, electronic, mechanical photocopying, documentary, film or in any other format without prior written permission of the publisher.

Extracts from the Authorized Version of the Bible (The King James Bible), the rights in which are vested in the Crown, are reproduced by permission of the Crown's Patentee, Cambridge University Press.

The Scripture quotations from the Revised English Bible (as indicated) are copyright © Cambridge University Press and Oxford University Press 1989, all rights reserved.

The Churchill quotation on page 20 is reproduced with permission of Curtis Brown, London on behalf of the Estate of Sir Winston Churchill, copyright © Winston S. Churchill.

Every reasonable effort has been made to trace the copyright holders of material reproduced in this book, but if any have been inadvertently overlooked the publisher would be glad to hear from them.

Sacristy Limited, registered in England & Wales, number 7565667

British Library Cataloguing-in-Publication Data
A catalogue record for the book is available from the British Library

ISBN 978-1-908381-22-4

Preface

It is no accident that the King James Bible is still read aloud today. The unsurpassed majesty of its prose flows naturally, both from the beauty of its translation, and from its cradle in the Jacobean era, making it important not only to Christians, but as the shared linguistic heritage of all English speakers.

In this short guide, everyday phrases found in the King James Bible are used to introduce the reader to each of the sixty-six separate books and letters that make it a whole. *The Writing on the Wall* thus covers a journey through some 3,000 years of belief in the single God and Creator of the cosmos, and the phrases become 'keys' to 'unlock' the Scriptures. As well as the general reader, this guide has been found useful by teachers, enthusiasts of the King James Bible and those interested in English as a foreign language, and as a ready reference to the contents of the Bible. Readers are encouraged to explore the Bible further, using an up to date translation. Some of the phrases originate in the King James Version (KJV) and others in earlier translations. Many of the phrases have changed in wording over time, and some may occur in several different books of the Bible. The total number of such biblical phrases may exceed three hundred, and a selection of these is included in an index.

The original version of this book was prompted by the 400th anniversary of the King James Bible and brought to fruition with encouragement from Canon Professor John Bowker. His book, *The Complete Bible Handbook* (1998), was a useful reference for my brief introductions and is still in print. Another helpful ingredient was the ground-breaking *Jesus and the Eyewitnesses* (2006) by Professor

Richard Bauckham, and some of the New Testament introductions reflect his findings. Thanks are also due to the Reverends John Proctor, now General Secretary of the United Reformed Church, and Dr Philip Jenson, Lecturer in Old Testament and Biblical Theology at Ridley Hall theological college, Cambridge, for casting their expert eyes over draft texts, and to Sacristy Press for bringing it to the wider public.

This book was originally produced as a successful fundraiser for my local church, 'St Mary's, Buckden: the A1 Church', which is situated beside the A1 trunk road, and consists of a beautiful Grade 1 listed medieval building and additional award winning modern facilities. Royalties from this published edition are being donated to help keep this modern facility open to journeyers at the point where the A1 passes through Cambridgeshire, providing rest and refreshment as sustenance for both body and soul. My hope is that many readers will discover a story which, with God's grace, will enrich their lives.

Richard Noble
December 2014

Contents

Preface iii

The Dedication to King James 1

The Old Testament 3
Genesis (The First Book of Moses) 5
Exodus (The Second Book of Moses) 6
Leviticus (The Third Book of Moses) 7
Numbers (The Fourth Book of Moses) 9
Deuteronomy (The Fifth Book of Moses) 10
The Book of Joshua 12
The Book of Judges 13
The Book of Ruth 14
The First Book of Samuel 16
The Second Book of Samuel 18
The First Book of the Kings 19
The Second Book of the Kings 20
The First Book of the Chronicles 22
The Second Book of the Chronicles 23
Ezra 24
The Book of Nehemiah 26
The Book of Esther 27
The Book of Job 29
The Book of Psalms 30
The Proverbs 31
Ecclesiastes, or The Preacher 33

The Song of Solomon, or Song of Songs 34
The Book of the Prophet Isaiah 36
The Book of the Prophet Jeremiah 37
The Lamentations of Jeremiah 38
The Book of the Prophet Ezekiel 40
The Book of Daniel 41
Hosea 43
Joel 44
Amos 46
Obadiah 47
Jonah 48
Micah 50
Nahum 51
Habakkuk 52
Zephaniah 53
Haggai 54
Zechariah 56
Malachi 57

The Intertestamental Period 59

The New Testament 60
The Gospel according to St Matthew 61
The Gospel according to St Mark 62
The Gospel according to St Luke 64
The Gospel according to St John 66
The Acts of the Apostles 68
The Epistle of Paul the Apostle to the Romans 70
The First Epistle of Paul the Apostle to the Corinthians 71
The Second Epistle of Paul the Apostle to the Corinthians 73
The Epistle of Paul to the Galatians 74

The Epistle of Paul the Apostle to the Ephesians 75
The Epistle of Paul the Apostle to the Philippians 76
The Epistle of Paul the Apostle to the Colossians 78
The First Epistle of Paul the Apostle to the Thessalonians 79
The Second Epistle of Paul the Apostle to the Thessalonians . . .81
The First Epistle of Paul the Apostle to Timothy 82
The Second Epistle of Paul the Apostle to Timothy 83
The Epistle of Paul to Titus 85
The Epistle of Paul to Philemon 86
The Epistle of Paul the Apostle to the Hebrews 87
The General Epistle of James 89
The First Epistle General of Peter 90
The Second Epistle General of Peter 91
The First, Second, and Third Epistles of John 92
The General Epistle of Jude 94
The Revelation of St John the Divine 95

Glossary 97

Index to idioms and phrases in the King James Bible 100

The Dedication to King James

Inestimable treasure
Things of profound and lasting value

The translation into English of the Bible, completed in 1611, was a publishing phenomenon. Earlier translations, such as those by William Tyndale in 1526 or Myles Coverdale in 1535, were suppressed or of limited circulation, but this one was promoted by the King and achieved worldwide circulation over the next four centuries. It is now known as the King James Version, and it has had a profound impact on most versions that followed and on the English language itself. The translators used many common English expressions of the time but, more importantly, new phrases translated *verbatim* from the original Hebrew and Greek texts entered into common speech as a consequence of the popularity of this version of the Bible. In the second paragraph of their dedication, the translators describe God's sacred word as that '*inestimable treasure*', their aim being 'to make God's holy truth to be yet more and more known' among those whom others 'desire still to keep in ignorance and darkness'. The collection of books that form the Bible is best understood not as the 'literal truth' of fundamentalists, nor as 'history' in its modern sense, but rather as writings by authors who, though having human limitations, wrote from their profound faith in God. Thus it should be no surprise that readers of the Bible today are able to relate its content to this modern world, and to find within it meaning and inspiration for their daily lives.

About the Phrase

In 2009, at the opening of the African Synod of the Catholic Church, Pope Benedict XVI said that Africa's deep sense of God was 'an *inestimable treasure* for the whole world' (*Vatican Information Service*, 5 October 2009). The words are currently used to describe the sacred music of the Latin mass, now in danger of being lost to posterity. *A Treasure of Inestimable Value* (2007) is the title of an album by the St Agnes Choir, New York, comprising Gregorian chant and other sacred music. The phrase is used of concepts beyond the bounds of language, such as the love of God.

The Old Testament
(excluding the Apocrypha)

Composition
The collection of Hebrew scrolls forming the Old Testament changed over time. The books and parts of books making up the King James Version of the Bible we know today form the Protestant Canon. Additional material from the Catholic Canon is in the Apocrypha. The first five books form the Pentateuch (or Torah) and, though titled as books 'of Moses' in the KJV, they cover a variety of styles and material, tracing the story of the Hebrew people up to the time when, as a 'nation' of tribes, they were ready to enter their 'promised land'. The next twelve books, from Joshua to Esther, tell the rest of the story. A group of five books follows: Psalms, the Song of Songs, and three which are known as 'Wisdom Books', namely Job, Proverbs, and Ecclesiastes. Next come the 'Major Prophets': Isaiah, Jeremiah plus his Lamentations, Ezekiel, and Daniel. Twelve books of the 'Minor Prophets' make up the rest of the Old Testament.

Chronology
The Bible begins with its stories of creation and develops into the family story of the Patriarchs in prehistory, leading to the exodus from Egypt. A United Monarchy of the Hebrew tribes was established under Saul, followed by King David and then King Solomon who built the Temple in Jerusalem. The kingdom split into Judah in the south and Israel in the north after the death of Solomon, with their principal cities of Jerusalem and Samaria. Israel fell to Assyria and Judah to Babylon (722 BCE and 586 BCE respectively), which resulted in a substantial portion of the population being cast into exile for many years. Some of them were allowed to return to Jerusalem in 538–432 BCE, during which time they rebuilt the

Temple. The Hebrew people of Samaria had their own version of the Pentateuch and did not accept Jerusalem as a centre of worship. The books of the prophets cover more than five centuries, with five of them relating events prior to the exile, Obadiah and Isaiah being from Judah, and Jonah, Amos, and Hosea from Israel.

Covenant
Central to the story is the way the Hebrews kept lapsing into idolatry with God showing mercy to the surviving 'remnants' of the faithful. Key to this relationship is the ancient concept of a legal covenant, made between God and his people in commitments such as those with Noah after the flood, with the patriarch Abraham, with the Hebrews under Moses, and with King David. These include sin, judgement, and punishment, but also promise and expectation. The Davidic hope of an eternal throne introduces the idea of the 'Messiah', Son of David, whose reign would embody peace, security, and everlasting justice, linking the Old Testament to the New.

Genesis (The First Book of Moses)

The Land of Nod
'Slumberland', where we nod off to sleep

The Bible opens with a vivid picture of Creation and a moral tale of humanity's origin, leading abruptly to murder when Cain kills his brother Abel. Cain is banished to wander in the *land of Nod* (4:16). Wandering people are a feature of the book. It is a treasure trove of stories reaching back into the obscurities of prehistory, but it also contains extraordinary insights into our human condition. In common with science, Genesis depicts mankind as a single human race. In common with most religions, it recognises a divine order beyond the material. For both Judaism and Christianity, this book is the foundation for belief in a single God of Creation, beyond human comprehension but claiming as his own those who are faithful in acknowledging him as Lord. These begin with Noah, followed by the patriarchs Abraham, Isaac, and Jacob, their offspring, 'the Children of Israel', and all who come after. The final chapters tell the amazing story of Joseph, his brothers' treachery, their eventual reconciliation, and the family's escape from famine to Goshen in Egypt.

About the Phrase
The pun associating the biblical Nod with the common English word 'nod' is probably first recorded in literature as a couplet of puns about going off to bed in Jonathan Swift's book, *A Complete Collection of Genteel and Ingenious Conversation* (1738):

> Col. Atwitt: I'm going to the *Land of Nod*.
> Neverout: Faith, I'm for Bedfordshire.

The Land of Nod is the title of a poem about dreams in *A Child's Garden of Verses and Underwoods* (1913) by Robert Louis Stevenson (1850–1894), and the name of a small hamlet at the end of a two mile long cul-de-sac in the East Riding of Yorkshire. There is a bedroom furniture store called *Land of Nod* and another called *Slumberland*.

Exodus (The Second Book of Moses)

An eye for an eye
Repaying wrong, like for like

The escape or 'exodus' of the Children of Israel from Egypt is a dramatic story that has inspired countless liberation movements. Though welcomed as refugees in Goshen at first, the Hebrews would become oppressed as slaves over the course of the following four hundred years. Key events are the emergence of Moses as their leader and the ten plagues suffered by the Egyptians (7:14–12:30), culminating in the Passover (12:1–36) and the dramatic escape from Egyptian bondage and crossing of the Red Sea. Forty years of desert wanderings follow in which two stone tablets are received by Moses on Mount Sinai bearing the Ten Commandments. These are later elaborated in the 'Book of the Covenant' (see 20:1–23:33) with a concept of retributive justice: 'then thou shalt give life for life, *eye for eye*, tooth for tooth' (21:24). But the Hebrews relapse into idol worship, and Moses' brother Aaron, now the high priest, makes them a golden calf (32:1–6). Moses establishes a tented

Tabernacle as a focus for worship while the Hebrews continue wandering in the desert (33:7).

About the Phrase
'*Eye for eye*, tooth for tooth' comes again at Leviticus 24:20 and at Deuteronomy 19:21. The principle of 'like for like' is very ancient—it even occurs in the oldest text ever deciphered, the *Code of Hammurabi* (*c.*1770 BCE, clause 196). It is the basis of the legal concept of *lex talionis,* the law of retaliation, which is the moral principle of proportional punishment that still underlies most criminal sentencing. The phrase as it is used today is from the New Testament, where Jesus upturns the concept of retributive justice with that of 'turning the other cheek':

> Ye have heard that it hath been said, An *eye for an eye*, and a tooth for a tooth: But I say unto you, That ye resist not evil: but whosoever shall smite thee on thy right cheek, turn to him the other also
> *Matthew 5:38-39*

Leviticus (The Third Book of Moses)

To be a scapegoat
Being made to bear the blame for others

When the Tabernacle (see page 6) was constructed to house the Ark of the Covenant, Moses gave the functions of serving as priests to his own tribe, the Levites, under the leadership of his brother

Aaron. This book deals with intricate laws on holiness, purity, rituals, sacrifice, fasts, and feasts. Holiness to the Hebrews involved a quest for purity, attained by the removal of every kind of sinfulness or uncleanness that might contaminate or separate them from God. Disrespect of holiness carried the danger of retribution, so God's name could not be uttered and holy things were the preserve of the priests. When Aaron's sons die, having sinned, he proceeds to 'cast lots upon the two goats; one lot for the LORD, and the other lot for the *scapegoat* . . . But the goat, on which the lot fell to *be the scapegoat*, shall be presented alive before the LORD, to make an atonement with him, and to let him go for a *scapegoat* into the wilderness' (16:8–10). Aaron confesses the wickedness and rebellion of his household and all the Israelites, while laying both his hands on the head of the *scapegoat*, who will take them away to a solitary place in the wilderness (16:20–22).

About the Phrase

Leviticus is the only book in the Bible where *scapegoat* appears, and, in fact, it only occurs in one chapter of this book (16:8, 10, 26). The concept of a *scapegoat* existed long before the emergence of monotheism and the theology of Atonement, or *Yom Kippur*, in Judaism. For Christians the means of Atonement, or being reunited with God, is the restorative Cross of Jesus Christ. The notion of a sense of guilt being transferred onto others has become so widespread in modern secular society that use of the word has become very common in speech and media titles. It is even used as a verb, '*scapegoating*', as in the singling out of political ringleaders as examples, or in the projection of uncomfortable thoughts and feelings onto others. Instances might be the persecution of Jews in Nazi Germany or the sidelining of well-performing workers by an under-performing majority. It seems humans are so uneasy with the guilt of sin that a vicarious route is needed to escape such feelings.

Numbers (The Fourth Book of Moses)

Peace offering
*A gift or service for the purpose of
procuring peace or reconciliation*

The appropriately named Numbers seems to be a catalogue of genealogies, head counts, laws, and ceremonials, but it covers a vital stage in the formation of the Children of Israel as a nation following their exodus from oppression in Egypt. Through forty years of wandering in desert lands they are led by Moses and his brother, Aaron. Their journey is a transition from a lack of faith in both their God and their leaders to a realisation of their destiny as God's people in preparation for entry into their promised land. The organisation of the many tribes and encampments is described, including the dedication of the altar with a massive sacrifice of 204 animals for the *peace offering* (7:84–89). Murmurings, outright rebellion, and treachery culminate in the betrayal of their God for a heathen idol. They suffer retribution and Moses is condemned never to enter the promised land. The book contains the familiar words: 'The Lord bless thee and keep thee; the Lord make his face to shine upon thee and be gracious unto thee; the Lord lift up his countenance upon thee, and give thee peace' (6:24–26).

About the Phrase
For the Hebrews, a *peace offering*, unlike its modern usage, was a specific sacrificial procedure in which the sweet smell from the burning fat of the sacrificed animal symbolised the peaceful coexistence of God, priest, and people. The term occurs eighty-five times in the Old Testament (KJV), including nineteen appearances in Numbers and twenty-nine in Leviticus. The biblical phrase *peace offering* is frequently used in common speech, news headlines, and book titles. Hector Hugh Munro (1870–1916), the mischievously witty writer better known as 'Saki', used *The Peace Offering* as a short story title in his macabre collection, *The Chronicles of Clovis* (1911).

Deuteronomy (The Fifth Book of Moses)

The apple of one's eye
The delicate pupil of the eye, used figuratively to describe a person or thing cherished above others

Deuteronomy is the last of the five books of Moses, the Pentateuch (see page 3). It covers the legal Covenant between the Children of Israel and God, their Lord, and is set in the plains of Moab prior to entering their promised land. Intricate laws ruling the lifestyle of the Hebrews are described, including a restatement of the Ten Commandments of Exodus (compare Exodus 20:1–17 to Deuteronomy 5:6–21). The phrase in question occurs in a poem near the end of the book known as the Song of Moses (32:1–43) which, in its breadth and originality of form, is unique in the Old Testament. God's faithful guidance of his people in safety through the desert wilderness to a rich and fertile land is contrasted with their corrupt ways, their lapse into unfaithfulness, and even the threat of national extinction. It relates how God found their ancestor, Jacob, 'in a desert land, and in the waste howling wilderness; he led him about, instructed him, he kept him as *the apple of his eye*' (32:10).

About the Phrase

Use of the word *apple* as a metaphor for the eye's delicate round pupil is very old, and the phrase with its figurative meaning appears in Old English in *Gregory's Pastoral Care*, attributed to King Aelfred the Great (885 CE), long before such use in translations of the Bible (see also Psalm 17:8, Proverbs 7:2, Lamentations 2:18, and Zechariah 2:8). Shakespeare used the expression with its literal meaning of the eye's pupil in *A Midsummer Night's Dream* (1594) in which Oberon, squeezing flower juice into Demetrius's eyes, says 'Hit with Cupid's archery/ Sink in *apple of his eye*' (Act 2, Scene 2). In contrast, the modern, figurative use of the expression comes straight from the Bible, as used by Sir Walter Scott (1771–1832) in his popular novel *Old Mortality* (1816): 'Poor Richard was to me as an eldest son, *the apple of my eye*.'

The Book of Joshua

Go the way of all flesh
To die, the natural ending of all life

The term 'The Law of Moses' (8:31–34) first occurs in this book. On a first reading, the trail of conquests, destruction of cities, and parcelling out of other people's lands might seem to portray a ruthless deity destroying all who stand in the way of his chosen people, but this is a one-sided view of the scripture. The essence of the book is in the people's faith (or lack of it), in stories about a weak people with divine help being able to defeat far stronger enemies, and in the extreme measures needed to avoid succumbing to idolatry. The Hebrews prosper when they keep clear of idolatry and intermarriage with the heathen population, but judgement and failure follow sin and unfaithfulness. Stories of note include Rahab and the spies, as well as the miraculous Jordan crossing and fall of Jericho (chs. 2–6). The Canaanites were not eliminated either in Joshua's time or afterwards, and the Hebrews had to live with their neighbours. The idolatry of selfish ends being placed before the good of others is the danger that produces acts of inhumanity throughout history. As Joshua approached death he said 'I am *going the way of all the earth*' (23:14).

About the Phrase
The phrase *The way of all flesh* does not appear in the Bible or in any of Shakespeare's works. But 'all flesh' is a biblical term denoting both humans and animals. The current idiomatic phrase carries connotations of both physical and moral decay. The Victorian novelist Samuel Butler (1835–1902) used the biblical expression (23:14 and 1 Kings 2:2) as the basis for the title of his satirical

novel, *The Way of All Flesh*, published posthumously in 1903. This semi-autobiography savaged the hypocrisy of Victorian domestic life and was a literary time-bomb of its day.

The Book of Judges

Ploughed with my heifer
Coercion of a person's wife

After the death of Joshua the tribes of Israel became established in their promised land, but they had no leader and failed to remove all the indigenous people with their heathen gods. The Law of Moses was forgotten, they worshipped idols, abandoned their God, and some even married into surrounding tribes. A series of judges emerged to bring order from chaos, and this book sees 'the Spirit of the Lord' as being either with or against them according to their success. Some stories about the judges are particularly prominent: for instance, that of Deborah, the only female judge of the Israelites (chs. 4–5). Similarly memorable is Gideon, who uses his legendary fleece to check if God will be with him and then defeats the Midianites (chs. 6–7). There is a macabre turn when Jephtha vows to offer God a burnt sacrifice of the first person he sees after defeating his enemy. To his great despair, the price of his victory is revealed to be his own daughter and only child (ch. 11). Chapters 14–26 cover the stories about Samson. In chapter 14, after killing a roaring lion, he embarks on his heroic acts, posing a riddle to his enemies the Philistines. He had, unfortunately, taken one of them as his wife, who then betrays him by giving them the answer. Samson asserts they would never have solved it 'if ye had not *plowed with my heifer*' (14:18).

About the Phrase
From ancient times ploughs were drawn by castrated bullocks and certainly not by a maturing female calf (heifer). Someone accused today of *ploughing with my heifer* might well grasp the meaning of this sexually loaded metaphorical expression immediately, provided they were familiar with the Samson story, or with farming animals. Samson's riddle that resulted in the phrase 'Out of the eater came forth meat, and out of the strong came forth sweetness' (14:14), was prompted by his discovery of bees and honey in the carcass of the lion he had killed. The last seven words of this quotation appear below an image of a rotting lion's carcass as a slogan on the UK worldwide product, *Lyle's Golden Syrup*. This is confirmed by *Guinness World Records* (2007) as the world's oldest instance of branding and packaging.

The Book of Ruth

Such a one
An unnamed person of a particular understood kind,
or of a kind that has been or is to be indicated

This short book tells a beautiful and moving story about the faithfulness and devotion of a Judean family in difficult circumstances. Famine at home in Bethlehem forces them to flee to the land of Moab and the sons marry Moabites. The men die and Naomi, the mother, bitter and with no prospects, returns to Bethlehem with Ruth, one of her Gentile daughters-in-law. Ruth finds favour with Boaz, who happens to be one of her mother's kinsmen. Naomi sees the opportunity of redeeming her husband's land through marriage. But there is a senior kinsmen who would have first option. Boaz waits to meet this potential redeemer, greets him: 'Ho, *such a one*' (4:1), and concludes a deal. Ruth and Boaz marry, and their son Obed is to be the grand-father of King David. The book is taken as an example of how the working out of God's purposes extends beyond his Covenant with the Children of Israel. Ruth is regarded as the great example of a Gentile woman becoming a Jew.

About the Phrase

Such a(n) one occurs twelve times in the KJV, in several of Shakespeare's plays, and as part of the title of *A Description of Such a One As He Would Love*, a poem by Sir Thomas Wyatt (1503–1542). In his articles about Cape Cod, H. D. Thoreau (1817–1862) describes a tragic loss of Irish emigrants in a shipwreck:

> Sometimes there were two or more *children*, or a parent and child, in the same box, and on the lid . . . written with red chalk, *Bridget such-a-one, and sister's child.*
>
> **Cape Cod, 1865**

In his poem *Locksley Hall* (1835), Alfred, Lord Tennyson (1809–1892) wrote:

> I remember one that perish'd; sweetly did she speak and move;
> *Such a one* do I remember, whom to look at was to love.

> Can I think of her as dead, and love her for the love she bore?
> No—she never loved me truly; love is love for evermore.

The First Book of Samuel

A man after one's own heart
Having the same opinions or interests as oneself

The priestly descendants of Aaron (see page 7) become increasingly corrupt, especially the two sons of Eli. Samuel, a Levite, was committed as a boy to work under Eli but then hears a direct call from God. Eli dies of shock when the Philistines capture the Ark of the Covenant and kill his sons (chs. 3–4). Samuel, by then a priest and prophet, keeps faith and becomes a judge of the Hebrew tribes. He discerns God's directions and, when the people agitate to have a king like the surrounding nations, he finds Saul and anoints him as king. Saul's reign is filled with battles against these neighbours, and the Ark is given back. Jonathan, Saul's heir, emerges as a champion in battle, but Saul disobeys God and is admonished by Samuel who tells him that God is seeking instead, as successor to the kingdom, *a man after his own heart* (13:14). The classic story of David and Goliath follows (ch. 17). David, shepherd boy and musician, is anointed by Samuel as the future king and he becomes close friends with King Saul's son, Jonathan. Disaster overtakes Saul when he seeks out the Witch of Endor and is told he is doomed (ch. 28). He is defeated in battle, and, when his three sons are killed, Saul falls on his sword (see page 22).

About the Phrase

Samuel's expression about God seeking *a man after his own heart* is quoted by Paul the Apostle in Acts 13:22. In Samuel Butler's 1898 translation of Homer's *Odyssey*, the phrase appears in Book IV, paragraph 8:

> Look, Pisistratus, *man after my own heart.*

Bernard Shaw (1856–1950) also uses this phrase in his play *Major Barbara* (1905):

> Undershaft: Professor Cusins you are a young *man after my own heart.*
> Cusins: Mr Undershaft: you are, as far as I am able to gather, a most infernal old rascal; but you appeal very strongly to my sense of ironic humour.
> **Act II, scene 2**

The expression *after one's own heart* is widely applied to all kinds of people and even, commercially, to things such as food and perfume.

The Second Book of Samuel

Put words in someone's mouth
To suggest that someone meant one thing when really they meant something else

The two books of Samuel started as one but Samuel does not feature at all in this second half. It covers the reign of David, the great musician, poet, warrior, and king, who unites the Hebrew tribes and moves the Ark of the Covenant to Jerusalem, which becomes the new nation's capital and centre of worship. It includes David's famous lament on the deaths of Saul and Jonathan, and his grief over the death of his own rebellious but popular son Absalom (1:19–27 and 18:33). Treachery and intrigue develop in King David's household. He becomes infatuated with the beautiful Bathsheba, sends her husband away to be killed in battle, and then marries her. Later, Absalom is banished by his father for murdering his half-brother, Amnon, in revenge for Amnon's having raped Absalom's sister, Tamar. David is tricked by his servant who concocts a story to secure Absalom's return: the servant finds a woman to tell it and *puts the words in her mouth* (14:1–25). Such events show how God's purposes can be fulfilled by god-fearing but fallible people. David's name is prophesied to be one of the greatest on earth with an everlasting lineage. It is his son Solomon, conceived in sin with Bathsheba, who will build the Temple in Jerusalem.

About the Phrase
A modern phenomenon is for film scriptwriters to *put words in the mouths* of celebrities for dramatic effect which become quoted as fact. For example, Deep Throat's famous advice to "follow the money" in *All the Presidents Men*—a 1976 film about the Watergate

scandal—was an invention. The expression also appears in Exodus 4:15, Deuteronomy 18:18, Isaiah 51:16, and Jeremiah 1:9, but, in these cases, the phrase signifies that such speech is inspired by God. Nowadays, the phrase is generally used to describe the distortion of someone else's words for manipulative purposes.

The First Book of the Kings

Sheep without a shepherd
People or things lacking leadership or direction

Kings, like Samuel, is one book but two scrolls. They describe the history of a spoiled hope as David's successors fail to hold together the Hebrew people. This part opens with a high drama about the succession, as Solomon is chosen in place of his older brother and King David then dies. During a period of thirteen years following consolidation of the kingdom, Solomon builds the Temple in Jerusalem, dedicates it with a grand ceremony, and then builds his royal palace. His kingdom thrives on foreign trade, raking in hoards of gold and silver but, despite his renowned wisdom, his reign, like those of his forebears, is flawed. He takes foreigners as wives and supports their heathen worship. After Solomon's death, the United Monarchy divides into Judah in the South and Israel in the North, each with its own king. The prophet Elijah wins a great contest against the prophets of Baal on Mount Carmel, and later settles the affair of Jezebel and Naboth's vineyard (chs. 18–21). The northern kingdom of Israel turns to the cult of Baal. Micaiah, a prophet, sees Israel 'scattered upon the hills, as *sheep that have not a shepherd*' (22:17), and the king of Israel dies in battle.

About the Phrase

This Bible metaphor for lack of leadership occurs six times in the KJV. It appears first in the Old Testament in Numbers 27:17, 'be not as *sheep which have no shepherd*', again at 2 Chronicles 18:16, twice in Ezekiel at 34:5 and 34:8, in Zechariah 10:2, and once in the New Testament in Matthew 9:36, where Jesus is said to have been 'moved with compassion on them [the people of Israel], because they fainted, and were scattered abroad, as *sheep having no shepherd*'. Churchill used the current phrase in a speech to the Royal Academy in 1953 'Without tradition, art is a flock of *sheep without a shepherd*', and it is the form used in most Bible translations today. Currently, the power of the tabloid press to undermine political and business leaders, coupled with the growth of social media, has introduced 'leaderlessness' as a means for ordinary people to drive political and social change. The 'Arab Spring' and the 'Occupy Wall Street' movement in New York are examples of this new phenomenon.

The Second Book of the Kings

Set/put one's house in order
To settle or organise one's affairs

The book opens with a sick king of Israel dispatching messengers to the prophets of Baalzebub. These messengers are challenged by Elijah and later consumed by fire. Elijah tells the king that for abandoning his God he will 'surely die' (2 Kings 1:4). Later, Elisha succeeds Elijah in a dramatic handover (2:1–18). Evil ways continue and the northern kingdom, Israel, falls to Babylon. Judah survives with its independence intact. When the prophet Isaiah enters the narrative, Judah has a good king, but he falls mortally ill and Isaiah prophesies, 'Thus saith the Lord, *Set thine house in order*; for thou shalt die, and not live' (20:1). But the king lives and naively shows some visitors from Babylon his hoards of treasure. Years later, successive kings of Judah turn to cult worship. After repeated incursions, the Babylonians return yet again and plunder Jerusalem's treasure hoard. They take away into captivity and exile all but the poorest citizens of Judah. The book ends with the exiled king of Judah freed from prison as a favoured guest of the king of Babylon, giving hope for the survival of David's line. But the era of kings is at an end and God's people are in captivity.

About the Phrase

This saying is repeated word for word at Isaiah 38:1. Nowadays it is often heard in the everyday sense that people should first *put their own house in order* before meddling in the affairs of others. At least four different books have the title *Set Your House in Order*. At a time when the USA was sending young black men and young white men to fight side by side in Vietnam, Martin Luther King, Jr lamented that, back home, they could hardly live on the same block together and that the US had not even '*put our own house in order*' (National Cathedral, Washington, D.C., on 31 March 1968). At the World Economic Forum in the Chinese city of Dalian, the Chinese Premier Wen Jiabao was reported as urging countries embroiled in the Eurozone debt crisis to *put their own houses in order* before expecting support from China (*Daily Telegraph*, 14 September 2011).

The First Book of the Chronicles

Fall on one's sword
Take the blame for a situation by resigning from a position of responsibility

The scrolls that concluded the Hebrew Bible, 1 and 2 Chronicles, cover much the same ground as the books of Samuel and Kings but were rewritten with significant differences. The chronicler appears to be writing at a time when Jerusalem had become the established centre of the Hebrew faith and the northern kingdom had long since fallen, its people by then being of little concern. The main thrust is a new presentation of the earlier records but from this new perspective, which is to say, showing the tendency for good kings to be rewarded by God with prosperity and success, while bad kings incur His wrath and suffer disaster. The book traces the destiny of God's people through to Saul, their first king who, wounded and beaten in battle and fearing an ugly death from the Philistines, begs his armour-bearer to kill him, 'But his armour-bearer would not; for he was sore afraid. So Saul took *a sword, and fell upon it*' (10:4); the armour-bearer promptly followed his master in this act. The last two chapters cover the reign of King David, leaving out all his sinful behaviour.

About the Phrase
Saul's suicide is recounted both here and at 1 Samuel 31:4–5. To *fall on one's sword* and die rather than face a humiliating and cruel death at the hand of the enemy is an act dating from ancient times and enters fourteenth-century Middle English in the Wycliffe Bible translations: 'Saul took his swerd, and felde theronne'. Some doubt surrounds the practicality of this method without an accomplice

to steady the sword. When in *Antony and Cleopatra* Shakespeare includes the stage direction *Falling on his sword* (Act IV, Scene 15), Mark Antony botches the job and fails to die until he sees Cleopatra, still alive in the next scene. To *fall on one's sword* can be viewed as honourable, cowardly, or desperate, and has thus become a favourite metaphor for journalists reporting resignations in today's rough and tumble of politics and high profile news.

The Second Book of the Chronicles

God save the king
God grant that he may be safe and righteous

This second half of Chronicles continues the theme of the first, presenting a different view of the period from Solomon, third king of the United Monarchy of Israel and Judah, to the time of Cyrus of Persia, who conquered Babylon and allowed the Hebrews to return from exile to Jerusalem to fulfil God's will and rebuild the temple, which will be seen as fulfilling a great prophecy of Isaiah (2 Chronicles 32:32, referring to Isaiah 44:26-28). In a gripping episode, Attaliah, the mother of a slain and evil king of Judah, seized power by killing off most of the royal line and reigned for six years. Meanwhile Joash, one of the princes, had been saved and hidden away by a priest, who later gathered sufficient forces to proclaim him king with a great ceremony and the shout of '*God save the king!*' (23:11). Attaliah came running on hearing the commotion, and was taken out and put to death with all her followers. Heathen practices were eliminated under the guidance of this priest. Joash reigned as a good king while the priest was still alive but was then led astray and, with the return of heathen practices, was defeated in battle.

About the Phrase
God save the king/queen is the first line of the British national anthem and comes straight out of the Bible. The words of this entreaty first appear in the Coverdale Bible of 1535. The exact phrase occurs eight times in the KJV of which this is the last. Some other national anthems contain similar pleas to God, but, unlike them, 'God save the Queen' derives its official status from custom and practice rather than official decree. The tune dates from the seventeenth century and has the distinctive rhythm of a sixteenth-century galliard dance. '*God save the king*' is said to have been a watchword used in the sixteenth century by sailors in the Royal Navy on night watch; the response being 'Long to reign over us'.

Ezra

God of heaven and earth
God of all that exists both seen and unseen

Ezra and the following book, Nehemiah, deal mainly with the rebuilding of the Temple in Jerusalem by some of the Hebrews, whom the Persians, now in control of the city, had allowed to return from exile in Babylon. An exchange of letters reveals that the indigenous people feel threatened by the rebuilding of the city walls and object to the ruling authority. The Hebrews, claiming they are servants of the *God of heaven and earth* (5:11), challenge the Persians to find the original decree which permitted them to rebuild their temple; this is duly rediscovered. The books of the Old Testament were originally written in Hebrew but this passage was in Aramaic (4:8–6:18), a language widely used in diplomacy at that time. The second part of the book is mainly about rebuilding the relationship between the Hebrews and their God. Ezra was a scribe familiar with the laws of Moses and he points out God's power over the Persians in giving the Hebrew remnant a chance to rebuild their nation. He castigates the people for taking foreign wives, demanding these should be divorced to keep the nation pure.

About the Phrase

Ezra 5:11 is the only place in the KJV where the precise phrase, *God of heaven and earth,* occurs. The phrase is used today as the title of a number of religious books, writings, and songs, and also of works in the modern fantasy genre. *Heaven* and *earth* come together in association with *God* in several other Bible verses, the most significant of which is the first verse of the KJV: 'In the beginning *God* created the *heaven and the earth*' (Genesis 1:1). The power of the phrase comes from the familiarity of this opening passage.

The Book of Nehemiah

Laugh to scorn
Ridicule with contempt

The book opens with an extensive confession of the sins of the Hebrews which had led to their exile in Babylon. It is narrated from the mouth of Nehemiah, a Hebrew official of the Persian king. He obtains authority to oversee the rebuilding of the walls of Jerusalem and the resettlement of the Hebrew people as they return from exile. A graphic description follows of the ruined city (2:11-18). When Nehemiah explains his plans to the indigenous people he notes that 'they *laughed us to scorn*, and despised us' (2:19), but his forceful and practical personality wins through. The law of the Torah is read out in public during a great ceremony lasting seven days, as a build-up to a renewal of the Covenant between the people and God (see page 10). Hebrew practises are re-established and marriage into the local non-Hebrew population is prohibited. This and the preceding book, Ezra, were originally a single volume. They were probably written in the fourth century BCE and narrate events of the fifth.

About the Phrase
The expression *laugh to scorn* also occurs in at least ten other places in the Old Testament: for instance, in Psalm 22:7, 'All they that see me *laugh me to scorn*: they shoot out the lip, they shake the head'. Christians believe this passage foretells the persecution of Jesus and it is quoted by Handel (1685-1759) in his famous oratorio *Messiah* (1742), II.27. In the Gospels, at Matthew 9:24, Mark 5:40, and Luke 8:53, Jesus is *laughed to scorn* at the prospect of raising to life the only daughter of Jairus, a ruler of the synagogue. The expression

was in wide use at the time of Shakespeare and is still employed today. A typical example can be found in *Macbeth* (c.1605):

> Be bloody, bold, and resolute; *laugh to scorn*
> The power of man, for none of woman born
> Shall harm Macbeth
>
> **Act IV, scene 1**

It occurs with double meaning in *As You Like It* (1599):

> The horn the horn, the lusty horn
> Is not a thing to *laugh to scorn*
>
> **Act IV, scene 2**

The Book of Esther

For such a time as this
Used to describe the unexpected but timely appearance of someone at a critical time in history

In this gripping narrative, Esther finds herself chosen as queen by the king of Persia, who was at first unaware she was a Hebrew. She had been brought up among the minority Hebrew community by a devoted relative named Mordecai, and when the king is tricked into issuing a decree in a scheme to exterminate the Hebrews, Mordecai urges Esther to plead with the king on their behalf, suggesting that perhaps she has become queen *for such a time as this* (4:14). At no small risk to her own life, Esther pleads with the king and, in a breath-taking sequence of events, the tables are turned on the perpetrator of the scheme, Haman, who is hanged on the very gallows he had set up for Mordecai. The story is commemorated annually in the important Hebrew festival of Purim. For Christians it illustrates how people throughout history have been used in the working out of God's purposes. The best way to appreciate the book is in a single session as it is a good read with just ten short chapters.

About the Phrase
The phrase *for such a time as this* has been used about the timely emergence of contemporary figures such as Martin Luther King, Jr, Nelson Mandela, and Barak Obama. *For Such a Time as This: A Renewed Diaconate in the Church of England* is the title of a 2001 report in which deacons are seen as a 'go-between' linking the formal Church and the needy, secular world of today, arguing that diaconal ministers come into their own at times of social change and cultural crisis. Current world upheavals and conflicts are seen by many as heralding a time when women, having gained higher roles in government and society, can play a conciliatory role in world affairs. When Betty Williams and Mairead Corrigan of Northern Ireland were awarded the Nobel Peace Prize in 1976, their grass-roots initiative seemed to be *for such a time as this*, although it was another twenty-two years before the Good Friday Agreement was reached in 1998.

The Book of Job

By the skin of one's teeth
Saved by the narrowest margin or in the nick of time

Apart from its prose introduction and ending, this book is all poetry. It is a vivid account of the consequences of a heavenly dispute in which Satan taunts God to let him test the faith of Job, a wealthy and god-fearing man whose fortunes seem to result from the Lord's good favours. Job suffers a series of devastating calamities which strip him of his children, his possessions, and his health. Although he suffers terribly, he survives: 'My bone cleaveth to my skin and to my flesh, and I am escaped with *the skin of my teeth*' (19:20). The attempts of his friends to comfort him by explaining his woes as God's punishment for sin make matters worse, leaving them, and all gloom and doom merchants in their wake, branded as 'Job's comforters'. When Job rejects their arguments and then appeals to God, his patience almost exhausted, he is confronted by his own insignificance compared to the vastness of God's creation. The suffering of innocent and righteous people, the merits of holding enduring faith in adversity, and the need to question misfortune are the central issues of this gripping scripture.

About the Phrase
The widely used form of this English expression, using 'by' in place of 'with', makes little sense because there is no skin on teeth. Job 19:20 KJV is an attempt, repeated from the Geneva Bible of 1560, to translate an obscure Hebrew text. Perhaps Job feels as if he has been flayed alive, with the skin of his body stripped off, leaving him only with the skin left on his teeth, which of course does not exist (or more simply he finds himself, like his teeth, with nothing).

Despite having no literal sense, the vividness of the expression has gained it a wide currency, as when people escape/survive/manage *by the skin of their teeth*.

The Book of Psalms

At one's wits' end
At the limit of mental resources, utterly at a loss

This collection of Hebrew sacred poetry spans seven centuries and comprises hymns of praise, devotions, and laments, known on its own as the Psalter (Greek *psalterion*). Many psalms bear the name of King David, and common themes include God's mercy, his deliverance, and his righteousness, along with the law, kingship, and priesthood. They cover the heights and depths of human emotions, and were used in temple worship. The psalms were not tied to particular Hebrew festivals and are still widely used today in Christian worship. The poetry is based on sense and rhythm rather than rhyme and metre, and is thus well preserved in translation. Two particular features are the use of refrains and parallelism, where the sense is repeated using different words. Psalm 107 exhibits such refrains (for example, verses 6 and 8, 13 and 15, 19 and 21, 28 and 31), the last in the context of God's deliverance of seafarers (23–27) and parallelism in the words 'They reel to and fro, and stagger like a drunken man, and are *at their wit's end*' (107:27). When Jesus miraculously calms the storm (Matthew 8:22–27), echoing this psalm, it is understood as a sign of his divinity. People who turn to their Bibles when lonely or in trouble can often be found with them open at the psalms.

About the Phrase
This is the only verse in the KJV where this phrase is found. Interestingly, in the Coverdale translation of 1535 (used for the Psalter in early versions of the *Book of Common Prayer*), it appears as *wittes ende*, both in this verse and twice in *Isaiah*. *Wit's End* or *Wits End* is the title of several songs and music albums. It is a common name for houses and places, and is even used for a board game. The phrase is often an expression of utter frustration or despair, as when a woman was reported to be *at her wits' end* after hiccupping for eleven years (*Daily Express*, 19 February 2014). The Scottish evangelist Oswald Chambers (1874–1917) said 'When a man is *at his wit's end* it is not a cowardly thing to pray, it is the only way he can get in touch with reality'. Indeed, it is rare for people not to pray as a last resort.

The Proverbs

Pride goes before a fall
Excessive confidence leads to calamitous choices

Many of the proverbs have parallels in ancient Egypt and Mesopotamia, despite the claim in the opening verse that Solomon is the author. Whereas most of the Hebrew Scriptures are focused on the 'salvation' activity of God in their history, this is a collection of wise sayings. God's wisdom is seen as the basis of all creation (3:19), and the concept that wise living flows from God is intrinsic to the whole book: 'The fear of the Lord is the beginning of wisdom: and the knowledge of the holy is understanding' (9:10). By modelling their lifestyles on Proverbs, the Hebrews sought a route to personal success and happiness. Many of these sayings resonate with human experience in every culture, and they have penetrated deep into the English language. A typical example, which uses poetic parallelism (see page 30) is: '*Pride* goeth before destruction, and an haughty spirit *before a fall*' (16:18). Throughout the Bible, *pride* is portrayed as a vice that leads to destruction, but this should not be confused with the benign use of the English word in the context of achievement and self-worth, particularly when fulfilling God's potential in one's life.

About the Phrase
The sense of this saying is well illustrated in the New Testament where Timothy warns about the dangers of an inexperienced person being 'lifted up with *pride*' on being promoted to high office (1 Timothy 3:6). The notion of hubris in the Greek tragedies, arrogant ambition leading to ultimate ruin, mirrors this sense of *pride*. In his two volumes on Hitler, the historian Ian Kershaw (1943–) gives the title *Hubris* to the first, describing Hitler's rise to power, and *Nemesis* to the second, about his role in World War II and eventual suicide; Nemesis is the spirit of divine retribution in Greek mythology.

Ecclesiastes, or The Preacher

Fly in the ointment
Trifling cause that spoils something good

The implication that King Solomon was the author of this book only comes in chapters 1 and 2. The Hebrew subtitle suggests these are not the writings of a king, and the style of the Hebrew text is consistent with that of a period some seven centuries after Solomon. The book consists of the philosophical musings of an old man who acknowledges the goodness of God's creation but, having not relied on God himself, finds most of his life meaningless. The viewpoint is that of a nonbeliever in life after death, as is the case with most of the Old Testament. The book is best known for the saying 'vanity of vanities, all is vanity' (1:2 and 12:8), but the Hebrew word has a meaning closer to the mist that evaporates at sunrise; human life being but a breath (Genesis 2:7). The idiom originates in the pithy verse: 'Dead *flies* cause the *ointment* of the apothecary to send forth a stinking savour: so doth a little folly him that is in reputation for wisdom and honour' (10:1). The writer finds that, in life, reward or punishment and success or failure do not correspond with being wise or foolish and righteous or wicked. Nevertheless, to live by the laws of God's goodness makes sense.

About the Phrase
The modern expression comes straight from this passage. However, it has lost its vivid sense of corruption, and is used for minor complications that upset things or a flaw in something that is too good to be true. This phrase is a good example of how a word-for-word translation from an ancient language can lead to a new idiom, its meaning becoming obscured over time. Today's hygiene

standards and sell-by dates ensure that ointments never become putrid. *Fly in the Ointment* is the title of a short story by D. H. Lawrence (1885–1930), and continues to be used in the title of many books and songs.

The Song of Solomon, or Song of Songs

Lily among thorns
Beauty amongst ugliness

The alternative titles come from the first verse which can be translated 'The song of songs from the one to whom peace belongs'; 'Solomon'/'Shlomo'/'shalom' meaning peace. This beautiful song cycle represents the very best of Hebrew poetry, ranging through the joys of love, fear of separation, and intimate longings, capturing the intensity of the feelings of a lover and his beloved: 'As the *lily among thorns*, so is my love among the daughters' (2.2). The sense of the poetry can be taken at face value with analogies of beauty in the natural world. Alternatively it can be understood as allegory, reflecting God's dealings with Israel or the love of Christ, either for his church or for a person's soul, as something of delicate beauty in a fallible world. The writings date back at least to the fourth century BCE and have been attributed to the Hebrew King Solomon, of the tenth century BCE, but the identity of the actual author remains unknown. The book might even be a collection of poems from different periods.

About the Phrase

The verse in Song of Songs (2:2) was used by a seventeenth-century Puritan minister in Boston, Lincolnshire to justify his practice of separating his congregation into *lilies* and *thorns*, and worshipping separately with the former group. This is described in chapter 6 ('As the *Lily Among Thorns*') of *American Jezebel* by Eve LaPlante (Harper, 2004), a fascinating book about Anne Hutchinson, a controversial pioneer of religious freedom, equal rights, free speech, and women's ministry, who emigrated to Boston, Massachusetts in 1634, helped found the Rhode Island settlement, and has even been called 'America's founding mother'.

Kateri Tekakwitha (1656–1680, canonised 2012), a Roman Catholic saint and a Mohawk of north-eastern America, was disfigured by smallpox and came to be known informally as Lily of the Mohawks. She was shunned by her tribespeople for converting to Christianity, and is said to have lain on a bed of thorns while praying for the conversion and forgiveness of her kinsmen. Her gravestone bears a Mohawk inscription meaning 'The fairest flower that ever bloomed among red men'. Many books are titled with this phrase, including one about Saint Kateri, the eponymous *lily among thorns*.

The Book of the Prophet Isaiah

No peace/rest for the wicked
Commonly said of those too busy to find peace

Isaiah is one of the most significant of the Old Testament books and can be divided roughly into three parts. Chapters 1–39 contain prophecies against foreign nations and the Hebrews' waywardness. Chapters 40–55 relate to a point during the exile in Babylon and renewed hope in God after defeat and humiliation. Chapters 56–66 deal with the situation after the return from exile and stress the importance of staying true to the law. The book ends with a vision of a new heaven and a new earth, with people gathered from every nation. Features of the book are the beauty and power of the poetry and the concept of 'righteousness': 'There is *no peace*, saith the Lord, unto *the wicked*' (48:22; 57:21). Of major importance to Christianity are four passages concerning 'The servant of the Lord' (42:1–4; 49:1–6; 50:4–9; 52:13–53:12). The first is quoted in the New Testament (Matthew 12:18–21), as are parts of the other three. In the fourth, the suffering servant prefigures the passion and death of Jesus, the Messiah, as 'atonement' for the sins of God's people (53:7–9). Isaiah envisions a time when wars will cease (2:4), the earth will be full of God's glory (6:3), a Messiah will be born (9:6–7), and former enemies will be at peace with each other (11:7; 65:25).

About the Phrase
This common phrase comes straight from the Bible, but the word 'peace' in the KJV (Hebrew 'shalom' meaning 'wholeness', 'peace', or 'delight') has become *rest* in the form popularised in 1930s America when Harold Gray (1894–1968) gave the title *No rest for the wicked* to one of his 'Little Orphan Annie' cartoon series. *No rest/peace for*

the wicked forms the title of a wide range of albums, songs, films, and books. 'Ain't *No Rest for the Wicked*' is a popular song by the Kentucky rock band Cage the Elephant where the phrase occurs repeatedly in a remarkably thoughtful and poetic set of lyrics.

The Book of the Prophet Jeremiah

A leopard cannot change its spots
No one can change their innate character.

Jeremiah lived through the reign of Josiah, king of the southern kingdom of Judah, only to see the kingdom's defeat by Babylon and the exile of its people, as he had prophesied. Some of the fleeing Judeans took him with them into Egypt, where he later died. His extensive writings date from the seventh century BCE, and appear to have been edited and rearranged over the years. Josiah's grandfather, reputedly a bad king, had turned his back on the Hebrews' one and only God with a relapse into idol worship. Jeremiah urges God's wayward people to give glory to the Lord before it is too late, likening them to a lewd woman who invites violation. He sees God's impending punishment as inevitable, for 'Can the Ethiopian *change* his skin, or the *leopard his spots*? Then may ye also do good, that are accustomed to do evil' (13:23). Although Josiah restored the worship of the Hebrew God alone to Jerusalem, it was too late. Six key passages, known as Jeremiah's Confessions, consist of anguished pleas to God both for understanding and to be understood, still as relevant today as then (11:18–23; 12:1–6; 15:10–21; 17:14–18; 18:18–23; 20:7–18).

About the Phrase

'A leopard can't (or *doesn't*) *change its spots*' is the colloquial and widely used saying derived from this Bible verse. It is a favourite of cynics who will not 'believe it till they see it'. But history is full of people who, following a transforming experience, have revolutionised their outlook, as with Paul, the New Testament apostle (see page 68). In a controversial book *How the Leopard Changed Its Spots: Evolution of Complexity* (1994), Brian Goodwin (1931–2009) challenges some of the evolutionary concepts of natural selection. Rudyard Kipling (1865–1936), in his *Just So Stories* (1902), tells a whimsical story inspired by this verse of a leopard and an Ethiopian, *How the Leopard Got His Spots*.

The Lamentations of Jeremiah

Give up the ghost
To die, give up the will to live, or stop functioning.

Although this book is ascribed to Jeremiah, it is not known who actually wrote it. Each of the five chapters is an anonymous poem, vividly describing the despair in Jerusalem after its conquest by the Babylonians around 586 BCE. The young inhabitants and lifeblood of the city had been taken captive, leaving a few priests, elders, and desperate mothers behind who '*gave up the ghost* in the city' (1:19). The writer describes them scratching around for food and even resorting to cannibalism (4:10). In the third poem the writer, though desolate, declares he will wait patiently since God is all he has and surely his love is not exhausted. Here are the well-known words about God's mercy that have given new hope to countless believers: 'new every morning: great is thy faithfulness' (3:21–24, 32). The poems question how God can abandon and punish his own people, but the final verses assert that the Lord reigns forever and beg him to restore them again as in the past (5:19–22).

About the Phrase
This expression has the sense of a person's soul or ghost (i.e., spirit) leaving them at death and predates the KJV. Shakespeare used it in *Julius Caesar*, Act V: Scene 1 and in *Henry VI: Part 3*, Act II: Scene 3. In the Old Testament it is used eight times in the simple sense of dying, but at Jeremiah 15:9 it has the sense of giving up the will to live. The phrase expresses the death of Jesus on the cross at Mark 15:37, 39, Luke 23:46, and John 19:30. It is used as a title for books, and, in her autobiographical memoir *Giving up the Ghost* (2010), Hilary Mantel (1952–) describes how she came to be childless, and how her life as a writer is infused by the ghosts of 'what might have been'. *Give up the Ghost* is the name of a hardcore punk band from Boston, Massachusetts which suddenly '*gave up the ghost*' in 2004. The band subsequently staged a number of reunion shows.

The Book of the Prophet Ezekiel

Wheels within wheels
Hidden influences, a complication of circumstances

Ezekiel was from a priestly family and received his call to prophesy during the exile in Babylon (2:1-3). Unlike some prophets, he valued temple worship, and his book is known for its oracles, ecstatic visions of God's glory, and layers of underlying significance. It opens with a vision of God's wide ranging, heavenly chariot throne with its all-encompassing wheels and all-seeing eyes: 'and their appearance and their work was as it were a *wheel in the middle of a wheel*' (1:15-21). He prophesies God's impending judgement and depicts Jerusalem as a promiscuous, adulterous wife (16:30-31; 23:19-21), as Hosea had done one hundred and fifty years earlier (see page 43). His tone softens when Jerusalem has fallen as he had prophesied (597/6 BCE), with the exiles in despair. He goes on to prophesy restoration and renewed prosperity (chs. 33-48); 'I will put my spirit within you . . . and you will be my people and I will be your God' (36:26-28). One of his best known visions is a dramatic picture of a valley full of dry bones that are breathed back into life by God's spirit. It is this powerful vision that is to become a basis for belief in life after death (37:1-15).

About the Phrase
With its wheels, Ezekiel's vivid yet obscure vision has helped give mystery to this metaphor. Arthur Miller (1915-2005) used the common expression, *wheels within wheels*, in Act 1 of *The Crucible* (1953) in the context of witchcraft. The expression frequently appears as a title for music and books, and as a headline for articles exposing intrigue in politics and society. *Wheels within Wheels,*

a 1933 novel by Alec Waugh (1898–1981), republished in 2012, describes how trivial acts in three far apart places can have far-reaching consequences. 'Like *a wheel within a wheel*' occurs as a dramatic phrase in the opening and closing verses of *Windmills of Your Mind*, a song performed by Noel Harrison (1934–2013) in the 1968 film The Thomas Crown Affair.

The Book of Daniel

The writing on the wall
Signs of impending disaster

Daniel is named as author in the text (9:2; 10:2; 12:4) but, apart from late writings in the Apocrypha, the name is virtually confined to this book. It is full of exciting stories and prophetic visions set in the Babylonian exile of the sixth century BCE, though many scholars date it much later. The Old Testament books were written in Hebrew, but five of Daniel's well-known stories (2:4–7:28) were in Aramaic: the burning fiery furnace, Nebuchadnezzar's dream, Belshazzar's feast, Daniel in the lion's den, and the dream about four beasts. These are thought to be prophecies of the successive empires of Babylon, Media, Persia, and Greece. In the third, King Nebuchadnezzar's son, Belshazzar, holds a feast and orders the sacred vessels of gold and silver, plundered from the Hebrew Temple (see page 21), to be brought as drinking cups for the guests and their concubines. Flushed with wine, they worship their heathen gods, whereupon the fingers of a disembodied hand begin to *write on the wall* of the palace the words '*mene mene tekel upharsin*' (5:5–25). Trembling with fear, Belshazzar summons his soothsayers, promising riches and power to whoever can interpret the ghostly message. When they fail, the queen remembers Daniel who had been appointed master of magicians by Nebuchadnezzar for his gifts of divination. Daniel agrees to decipher the writing but dismisses any notion of reward, and berates Belshazzar for profaning the sacred vessels by worshipping false gods. After reminding Belshazzar of how his father had been overwhelmed by pride, deposed and reduced to the state of an animal, Daniel interprets the menacing message: Belshazzar's days are numbered. He has been weighed in the balance and found wanting; Babylon will be divided between the Medes and Persians.

The book has had a profound influence on the New Testament, and Jesus used the phrase 'Son of Man', found in this book at 7:13–14, to describe himself (Mark 9:31). Of all the Hebrew books, Daniel is the most explicit on the resurrection. Its overriding themes are faithfulness in an alien land and fulfilment in the future. In Christianity this is realised in Jesus as Messiah. Passages on the last days have been, and still are, a source of frustrated speculation.

About the Phrase
The idiom comes straight from Daniel 5:5 and is often used in prose, lyrics, journalism, films, and videos, especially as headlines and titles. People who 'cannot read *the writing on the wall*' are like those who 'bury their heads in the sand'. In *An Autobiography or the Story of My Experiments with Truth* (1927), Mahatma Gandhi (1869–1948) warns that man will be reduced to the state of the beast if no one heeds *the writing on the wall*. The phrase appears in an unpublished poem by Jonathan Swift (1667–1745), entitled 'The Run Upon The Bankers'. Seen as somewhat prophetic, the poem was printed in 1734 following a Dublin banking crisis and contains the following lines:

A baited banker thus desponds,
From his own hand foresees his fall,
They have his soul, who have his bonds;
'Tis like *the writing on the wall.*

Hosea

Sow the wind, reap the whirlwind
Suffer the distressing consequences of a bad action in the past

In this vivid prophetic narrative, Hosea, a contemporary of Isaiah, marries a prostitute, Gomer, and uses her infidelity to illustrate the unfaithfulness of God's people in breaking the Covenant. In the Hebrews' covenant with God (see page 10), as in all ancient covenants, the overlord, God, promises to protect his vassals, the Children of Israel, on condition of their full allegiance, observing a secure family life, honouring parents, marriage, neighbour, and property. Using the strongest language possible, he rails against their idolatrous practices, warning them they will become captives of their heathen neighbours: 'Israel hath cast off the thing that is good . . . of their silver and their gold have they made them idols . . . mine anger is kindled against them . . . For they have *sown the wind*, and they shall *reap the whirlwind*' (8:3–7). Despite his use of such dramatic imagery to denounce their transgressions, Hosea describes God as a devoted parent with deep concern for the future of his chosen people. Thus Hosea's own faithfulness to Gomer, his undeserving wife, mirrors God's faithfulness.

About the Phrase
Reap the Whirlwind is the title of a novel by Geoffrey Bing (1968), another by David Mack (2007, as part of the *Star Trek: Vanguard* series), and of a work about the Lancaster Bomber by Martin Bowman (2012). Following the blitz of World War 2, Sir Arthur 'Bomber' Harris said in a famous speech which ultimately led to the controversial area bombing of Dresden civilians in 1945: 'They *sowed the wind*, and now they are going to *reap the whirlwind*'. Sowing and reaping are common themes in the Bible (see Haggai 1:6 and page 55, Galatians 6:7–8, and 2 Corinthians 9:6) and have become common metaphors. When Charles Goodyear, the inventor of industrial rubber, had lost both his patent battle and any benefit from his process he reflected ungrudgingly, 'Man has just cause for regret when he *sows* and no one *reaps*' (*A Centennial Volume of the Writings of Charles Goodyear and Thomas Hancock* (The American Chemical Society, 1939), p. 97).

Joel

Locust years
Years wasted through missed opportunities or hardship

Nobody knows who Joel was or when the book was written, but its importance lies in key prophecies that are taken up by later writers, reflecting on how God will save his people. Joel describes destruction by drought and a terrible plague of locusts. Next he visualizes a relentless army wreaking devastation far worse than the locusts. These are taken as portents of the 'day of the Lord', but

God 'is gracious and merciful, slow to anger and of great kindness' (2:13). Next is a theme of restoring 'the *years* that the *locust* hath eaten' (2:25), a concept of hope through which God will restore both people and their years of wasted failure. Joel's great prophecy follows (2:28): 'And it shall come to pass afterward, that I will pour out my spirit upon all flesh; and your sons and your daughters shall prophesy, your old men shall dream dreams, your young men shall see visions'. When, in the New Testament, God's Holy Spirit is poured out on Jesus' disciples (Acts 2:16), thousands from many nations become believers and Peter claims the event as the fulfilment of this prophecy.

About the Phrase
The Locust Years is the title of chapter 5, volume 1, of Churchill's *The Second World War* (1948), which deals with the years 1931 to 1935. In a parliamentary speech, he praised Sir Thomas Inskip for using Joel 2:25 to depict the dangers faced and the years wasted while the ineffective authorities, *the locusts,* allowed Britain to lag behind German rearmament (*Hansard*, vol. 317: 1101, 12 Nov 1936). *The Locust Years* has been used as a song title by Jerry Lee Lewis and by The Hammers of Misfortune. The concept of the *years* the *locusts* have eaten being redeemed has become a theme in Christian-based movements to reconcile nations and in restorative justice, such as when a reformed criminal uses past experience to help others turn away from a life of crime.

Amos

Can two walk together, except they be agreed?
*Not a phrase or idiom but an epigram aimed
at the root of human cooperation*

In common with Hosea, this book dates from the eighth century BCE and is older than later prophets, such as Jeremiah and Ezekiel, which come earlier in the Bible. Amos, a shepherd in eighth century BCE Judea, became a prophet in the northern kingdom of Israel, which was soon to fall (see page 21). He aroused the wrath of the people and the threat of expulsion by denouncing their king. He employs many agricultural images and makes an impassioned plea for social justice using a sequence of rhetorical questions. He accuses the people of transgressing the most basic demands of the law by abusing the poor, perverting the course of justice, disregarding their neighbours, and ignoring the Sabbath. His question, '*Can two walk together except they be agreed?*' (3:3), is part of this rhetoric and implies that the authority of his words comes from his close walk with God. The fifth chapter contains the earliest references in writing to a 'day of the Lord', a concept which develops through scripture into a day of divine, apocalyptic judgment at the end of the world.

About the Phrase
An obvious reply to the question '*Can two walk together, except they be agreed?*' is 'No, of course not', since without agreement they go their separate ways, and, consequently, this verse has been used as a title for books about marriage. In the past, the verse has been misused as justification for major schisms in the Church but, with more enlightened thinking, the mediating principle of agreeing

to disagree while remaining open to reconsideration is essential to peace, reconciliation, and unity. Two can indeed walk together once they have agreed to disagree.

Obadiah

Do as you would be done by
The 'golden rule': do to others as you would have others do to you.

In the first part of this, the shortest book in the Old Testament, Obadiah rebukes the Edomites. The Kingdom of Edom neighboured Judah and, like its inhabitants, claimed descent from Abraham. The Edomites were complicit in the Babylonian invasion, and so Obadiah warns them that 'as thou hast done it shall be done unto thee' (1:15). Although close to the popular phrase, these words convey the essence of just judgement. In the New Testament Jesus builds on the notion with a positive, forward looking exhortation: 'whatsoever ye would that men should do to you, do ye even so to them' (Matthew 7:12; Luke 6:31), describing a heavenly Father who gives good things to those who ask and do likewise. Obadiah's oracles of judgement on surrounding nations can be viewed as coming to fruition over ensuing centuries and as foreseeing a time of salvation or 'day of the Lord' when all creation honours the one and only God.

About the Phrase

The term 'golden rule', dates from the years after the KJV was published, and it is known as the 'ethic of reciprocity' in the social sciences. It is a key principle in each of the major world religions. When such an idea transcends the boundaries of race and religion, tribe and nation it becomes a cornerstone of peaceful coexistence. The expression *do as you would be done by* is first recorded in a letter to his son by The Earl of Chesterfield in 1747. The retributive words in Obadiah and the positive words of Jesus are contrasted by the behaviour of two characters in a Victorian moral tale for the young by Charles Kingsley, *The Water Babies* (1863). Mrs *Bedonebyasyoudid* reflects the *lex talionis* (see page 7) in contrast with the considerate Mrs *Doasyouwouldbedoneby*. The book was immensely popular in its day but, in common with many others, has fallen from favour as a children's classic on the grounds of its sometimes problematic nineteenth-century prejudices.

Jonah

Better to die than to live
Behind these words is the notion that death is
preferable to a life bound by shame or cowardice.

This is a vivid story of epic proportions recounted in only four short chapters. Jonah believes God requires him to preach destruction to the wicked and foreign city of Nineveh. He is so averse to becoming a prophet that he disobeys God and sails away on a ship for Tarshish. After his near-shipwreck and three days in the belly of a great sea monster, he eventually goes to Nineveh, prophesies against it and waits to see its destruction. When the inhabitants repent and God relents, Jonah is so angry that he begs God to kill him 'for it is better . . . *to die than to live*' (4:3). Jonah sits and waits to observe the fate of the city and is delighted when a vine grows up to shade him. When this is devoured by a worm, exposing him to the midday sun, he is furious and repeats the sentiment (4:8). His initial fear is borne out, that God in his mercy would spare the wicked city, negating his prophecy. This pivotal book presents the character of God as both judgemental and gracious, 'slow to anger, merciful and of great kindness' (4:2). Jesus points to Jonah's three days in the sea monster as a sign of his impending death and resurrection, and to Nineveh's repentance as a judgement on his current times (Matthew 12:39–41).

About the Phrase
The notion occurs in several sayings, as in the motto of the Royal Gurkha Rifles: *Better to die than live* a coward. Frederick Douglass wrote in his magazine, *Douglass's Monthly*: '*Better* even *die* free, *than to live* slaves' (March 1863). The Mexican revolutionary Emiliano Zapata (1879–1919) famously said that it is *better to die* on your feet *than live* on your knees. This noble sentiment lies behind the deaths of innumerable martyrs, but, in cases of utter despair or dismal failure, the sentiment has led to many a tragic suicide.

Micah

Swords into plowshares
A metaphor for the transition from weapons of war to the peaceful uses of technology

This book dates from the late eighth century BCE and has some of the most familiar passages in the Hebrew Bible. Micah was a contemporary of Isaiah and Hosea, and is the only prophet to whom words are attributed by another (compare 3:12 and Jeremiah 26:18). Micah was not at all popular (2:6–11), for he predicted ruin for the nation, accusing the rich of oppressing the poor, the leaders of corrupting justice, and the state prophets of being blind to the sins of their paymasters. He prophesied: 'they shall beat their *swords into plowshares,* and their spears into pruninghooks: nation shall not lift up a sword against nation, neither shall they learn war any more' (4:3). Using the terms of a law suit, Israel is accused of breaking God's Covenant. Heaven and Earth are appointed judges, defence is refuted, and sentence of destruction is passed. Micah specifies the duty 'to do justly, and to love mercy, and to walk humbly with thy God' (6:8). A new ruler will come out of Bethlehem in Judea with ancient origins (5:2) and God will 'turn again and have compassion on us', thus fulfilling his Covenant with Abraham (7:19–20).

About the Phrase
This prophecy of future universal peace (4:3) has wide appeal in a war-torn world, both in popular culture and for politicians (see also Isaiah 2:4, 65:25). The phrase *swords into ploughshares* has been used by two US Presidents: Eisenhower and Reagan. A bronze sculpture with the inscription 'Let Us Beat *Swords into Plowshares*' was presented to the United Nations by the Soviet Union in 1959

to symbolise the human need for peaceful produce to supplant weapons of war. The notion appears as a refrain in the *Greenham Common Women's Peace Camp Songbook*. The camp was established in 1982 to protest at nuclear weapons, being sited at RAF Greenham Common in Berkshire, England, and was the first of many.

Nahum

Slow to anger
A virtue of overwhelming worth in personal relationships and world affairs

Unlike some of the other prophets, Nahum vents his wrath against a foreign power, Nineveh, rather than his own people. Neither he nor his people have been identified, but the city of Nineveh is also featured in the book of Jonah (see page 48) and was the capital of Assyria until its fall in 612 BCE. In prophesying Nineveh's downfall, Nahum censures its tyranny, corruption, and wickedness. He declares God's universal sovereignty over all nations and their destinies. He asks: 'Who can stand before his indignation? And who can abide the fierceness of his anger?' (1:6). But the book can also be read on a cosmic scale, with Nineveh a symbol of everything that opposes God's supreme power and just purposes for the world. Nahum sees God as all-mighty but also as *'slow to anger'* (1:3); 'The Lord is good, a stronghold in the day of trouble; and he knoweth them that trust him' (1:7). The book includes the prophecy of a future saviour which also occurs in the book of Isaiah: 'behold upon the mountains the feet of him that bringeth good tidings, that publisheth peace' (1:15; see also Isaiah 52:7).

About the Phrase
Proverbs 14:29 (KJV) says: 'He that is slow to wrath is of great understanding: but he that is hasty of spirit exalteth folly'. The phrase *slow to anger* appears eight times in the Bible, usually as an attribute of God. It has been used as a popular song title and is commonly used as an exhortation or desirable attribute, often coupled with the words 'and quick to forgive'.

Habakkuk

Swifter than leopards
An expression conveying incredible speed

Habakkuk was a contemporary of Jeremiah and lived at the end of the seventh century BCE during the reign of Judah's King Josiah. He may well have survived to see his prophecies come true when Judah was invaded by the Babylonians. The first half of the book is a dialogue with God, in which Habakkuk admits the wayward ways of his people but cannot understand how a just and all-powerful God first does nothing and then proposes to punish them by the agency of Babylon, a terrible and dreadful nation, worse than themselves: 'Their horses also are *swifter than the leopards*, and are more fierce than the evening wolves' (1:8). God's answer is that they, in due course, with their arrogance and worthless idols, will be destroyed as nations exhaust themselves in vain: 'For the earth shall be filled with the knowledge of the glory of the Lord, as the waters cover the sea' (2:14). The third chapter is in the form of a prayer, to be sung to music in worship, which pleads for mercy and acknowledges God's mighty power.

About the Phrase
Leopards are now becoming increasingly rare, but the *swiftness of the leopard* was proverbial in the lands where they existed. At around sixty miles per hour, the speed of a leopard is marginally slower than that of a cheetah, the species which holds the speed record for a land animal. It is related in *The Two Babylons* (1903), a discredited book by Alexander Hislop, that the Christian historian Paulus Orosius (c.375–420) reports a leopard being sent by the King of Portugal to the Pope, and that its speed in overtaking and killing deer and wild boars elicited great astonishment.

Zephaniah

Put to shame
Cause to suffer humiliation or disgrace

This book, like Habakkuk and Nahum, was probably written at the end of the seventh century BCE. Unlike those prophets, Zephaniah claims royal descent and shows a keen awareness of state affairs. Proclaiming God's judgement, he accuses priests of polluting the sanctuary, the people of idolatry, and the princes and kings of complacency. His high birth makes this onslaught against the rich and powerful particularly significant. Jerusalem, Judah, and all the nations around will be punished, and he prophesies a 'day of the Lord' when everyone and everything will suffer a sudden and terrible end, when neither wealth nor power will save them. He urges those who live humbly to seek righteousness and humility as they may find shelter on that day (2:3). A remnant of Israel will be saved and God 'will get them praise and fame in every land where they have been *put to shame*' (3:19).

About the Phrase
The phrase *put to shame* is used thirteen times in the 1535 Coverdale Bible, and also occurs in the KJV at Judges 18:7, Isaiah 54:4, seven times in Psalms, and twice in Proverbs. Nonetheless, it does not seem to have been a common phrase as Shakespeare did not use it at all. Four centuries later, however, it appears nearly fifty times in the New International Version and over seventy times in the English Standard Version. This seems to be a good representative case of a common English phrase entering the language from translations of the Bible and being used more and more as the years go by.

Haggai

A bag with holes
Wasted purpose

This, the second shortest book of the Old Testament, dates from c.520 BCE, roughly coinciding with the reign of Darius, King of Persia. The Persians had, by this time, already given permission for the rebuilding of the Temple in Jerusalem. Haggai castigates his fellow citizens for building houses for their own safety while leaving the Temple in ruins. They have wasted their efforts as if sowing much but reaping little 'and he that earneth wages earneth wages to put it into *a bag with holes*' (1:6). He urges them to turn from their self-interested, troubled, and unsatisfied lifestyle to give priority to God and get on with the rebuilding efforts. Another theme in the book is the blessing that will follow obedience. God will keep his Covenant, his spirit will remain with his people (2:5), and his house will be full of peace and glory with the coming of the Messiah: 'it is a little while, and I will shake the heavens, and the earth, and . . . all nations, and the desire of all nations shall come' (2:6–7). It ends with God's predicted judgement on the heathen nations, with the mutual destruction of both themselves and their instruments of war (2:22).

About the Phrase
This phrase seldom penetrates into secular usage, but the folly of earning good money only to put it in *a bag with holes* and lose it is so graphic that the metaphor is common in Bible-based moral teaching and exhortation, especially in North America. Someone's folly or 'the devil's deceit' might be likened to *a bag with holes*. Typical rhetorical questions might include 'Does your *bag* have *holes*?' or 'Does the *bag* of your life have a *hole* in the bottom?'

Zechariah

The ends of the earth
The remotest extent of the world's land masses

The writings of Zechariah (520 BCE), both priest and prophet, follow straight on from those of Haggai. The completion of the rebuilding of the Temple, as recorded in Esra 6:15, was around this time. The contents of the book are rather obscure, but they consist of visions and prophecies that point to the coming of the Messiah, the sacking of Jerusalem (12:1–3; 14:1–2), and the end of the world. The central message is the proclamation of peace to all the nations, and a rule extending from sea to sea and to *the ends of the earth* (9:10). Prophetic verses of particular interest are: Jerusalem as a centre for all nations to seek and entreat the 'Lord of hosts' (8:20–23); a king coming in humility, riding on a donkey (9:9); the thirty pieces of silver being paid to a potter (11:12–13); and the scattering of the sheep following the striking down of the shepherd (13:7). Christians understand these Old Testament texts as pointing towards the following New Testament events: the metaphorical 'New Jerusalem' (Revelations 21:1–10); Jesus' entry to Jerusalem (Matthew 21:6–8); the potter's field bought by Judas with the money gained from betraying Jesus (Matthew 27:9–10); and the abandonment of Jesus by his disciples, of which Jesus himself had warned, quoting this very verse in Zechariah (Mark 14:27).

About the Phrase
Caxton used *Ends of the earth* in his translation of Jacobus de Voragine's *Golden Legende* in 1483 but, as with so many of the biblical phrases that only became current in the English language after the KJV, it does not appear in the works of William Shakespeare,

virtually complete by the time of its publication. The expression *the end/s of the earth* is repeated over forty times in the KJV Bible, especially in Job, the Psalms, Isaiah, and Jeremiah. Salvation by the Messiah, reaching *to the end/s of the earth* is declared in the Old and New Testaments, at Isaiah 49:6 and 52:10 and then mirrored at Acts 13:47. Books, ranging through many genres, use the phrase as a title. In the present age, with views from space showing earth as a globe without *ends*, it may seem odd that the phrase still commands such currency. The fact that it does so is witness to the lasting influence of the King James Bible.

Malachi

Refiner's fire
The lessons of life through which a person's character can be refined

Malachi comes at the end of the Old Testament in the KJV which uses the Protestant Canon, but it predates the time when collections of writings such as Chronicles, Psalms, and Proverbs were put together. Malachi presents his hearers with a series of challenging questions and unwraps each of them in turn with a pithy exposition of a prophetic theme. Two such themes are the basis of love and obedience, first in the Covenant between God and his people, and second in a marriage contract between two people. The coming of God's 'messenger of the covenant' is prophesied with the question 'who shall stand when he appeareth? For he is like a *refiner's fire*' (3:1–2). Christians understand this messenger as Jesus Christ, Incarnation of the one and only God. The Apostle Peter refers to 'faith . . . tried with fire'—the trial of faith through temptation—as being even more precious than refined gold (1 Peter 1:7).

About the Phrase
The familiarity of this phrase owes much to Handel's inclusion of Malachi 3:2 in Part 1 of his famous oratorio *Messiah* (1742) and '*Refiner's Fire*' being the popular title for the aria concerned. The phrase is also used in the title of a large number of books and music albums, mainly of a religious nature. In Malachi 3:3, it is written of God's 'messenger' that 'he shall sit as a refiner and purifier of silver . . . and purge them as gold and silver'. The story is told of a Bible study group who go to watch a refiner at work so as better to understand this scripture. The refiner sits with his eye steadily fixed on the crucible of silver lying in the hottest part of the flame while the impurities burn away. He explains he has to remove it at just the right moment, otherwise it is spoiled. When asked how he judges this moment he replies 'Oh, that's easy: when I see my image reflected in it.'

The Intertestamental Period

Between the last minor prophet and the birth of Jesus Christ, the face of the eastern Mediterranean and the Middle East was transformed by the conquests of Alexander the Great (356–323 BCE), establishing Greek as the main language of administration and culture in many regions. To the Jews, he gave semi-independence and allowed Jerusalem to retain its temple worship. The rump of his empire was later ruled by Antiochus IV Epiphanes ('God Manifest', 215–164 BCE), who provoked a Jewish rebellion in Jerusalem and carried out a huge slaughter of retribution. He struck at the heart of their faith by setting up idols in the Temple sanctuary and demanding to be worshipped as a god. This led to the Maccabean revolts and the purge of idolatry. Peace was eventually negotiated (155 BCE) and power later passed to the Romans, but Judah remained a dependent territory. Jewish people were active traders who established settlements and synagogues around the Mediterranean and in what is now Turkey. Many local people were won over by their monotheistic faith and became Jewish proselytes. Herod the Great was of Jewish proselyte stock and curried favour in Rome, where he was appointed 'King of the Jews'. He took control of Jerusalem (37 BCE) and reinforced his rule with huge building projects, such as the port of Caesarea and the Jerusalem Temple enlargement. The primary spoken language of the region had become Aramaic by this time. Judah had been split into the provinces of Judea and Galilee. This is the background to the birth of Jesus Christ around 6 BCE. Herod's death followed two years later.

The New Testament

This is the amazing testimony of God's intervention in human affairs through his Son, Jesus Christ, who would not be recognised as king of an earthly domain but of God's eternal kingdom. The four Gospels are followed by the Acts of the Apostles, which is a continuation of Luke's Gospel and introduces Paul the Apostle. In a series of missionary journeys, Paul takes Christianity to the Greek-speaking world. The following letters, mostly by Paul, are very early Christian records. The New Testament concludes with an extraordinary book of powerful visions that reveal Christ with God in glory, but in terms that are beyond normal human comprehension. During the twentieth century, the ascendancy of science over religion as the means of understanding the human condition, coupled with questions of how a benign God can allow such terrible devastation through human and natural causes, led to a decline in faith. In this century, the twenty-first since the Incarnation, with a growing awareness of world religions and realisation of a dimension in the human psyche that seems to transcend rational explanation, the scepticism of the recent past is dissolving. Each scientific discovery seems to reveal yet another layer of unknowns. The idea of human allegiance to a higher realm or 'God' as the basis of a meaningful life seems to be gaining ground once more, and Christians find that, in Jesus Christ of the New Testament, God is revealed in terms that can be grasped as a reality by the human psyche.

The Gospel according to St Matthew

Cast pearls before swine
Give things of value to those who will neither understand nor appreciate them

This gospel is traditionally regarded as being the work of Matthew the tax collector, apostle and disciple of Jesus. His native languages would have been Aramaic and Hebrew, but some scholars think this book may have been composed in Greek using Matthew's material. Used in Christian worship from earliest times, it is addressed to both Jews and Gentiles, reflecting an era when the Church was relating in new ways to its Jewish roots. Distinctive features are the emphasis on Jesus as Christ the King, the Messiah foretold by the prophets in fulfilment of the Hebrew scriptures, and on God's laws and promises being widened to include all humankind. 'Gospel' means 'good news', and Matthew relates the nativity of Jesus in this context with his ministry heralded by John the Baptist (chs. 1–3). He groups the teachings of Jesus together in 'The Sermon on the Mount' (chs. 5–7), commencing with 'the Beatitudes' (5:3–16) and emphasising the need for genuine, humble, and generous attitudes. He portrays Jesus as a radical teacher inviting rigorous obedience, but warning against hypocrisy in judging others, aiming at those who attempt to follow the letter of the Law of Moses while being blind to their own flawed attitudes. These teachings include 'Give not that which is holy unto the dogs, neither *cast ye your pearls before swine*, lest they trample them under their feet, and turn again and rend you' (7:6). Matthew's account of Jesus' life, death, and resurrection largely follows that of Mark (see page 62) and ends with his 'Great Commission' to make disciples of all nations, baptising in the name of Father, Son, and Holy Spirit.

About the Phrase

This common metaphor comes straight from the Bible. On 16 September 1938, in the *The Spectator*, Robert Carter reported a spiky exchange between two society women: 'Age before beauty, Mrs Parker', 'And *pearls before swine*', retorted Mrs Parker, sweeping in. Like so many colourful biblical phrases, this one is used very widely as a media title, in particular for a widely distributed, controversial American cartoon strip which first appeared in 2000. This is just one of many idiomatic phrases found in Matthew's Gospel in the KJV; indeed, the Gospel of Matthew is the source of more idioms than its three companions (see Index). This could corroborate some early references that Matthew's Gospel was composed in Hebrew rather than Greek. The Hebrew and Aramaic languages are rich in idiom and metaphor, unlike Greek, the original language of most of the New Testament texts. Indeed many of the much-used biblical phrases quoted in this book owe their existence to the word-for-word translation that King James' editors made from the Old Testament Hebrew texts (see page 1).

The Gospel according to St Mark

Measure for measure
In life one gets what one deserves

This Gospel is thought to be the work of John Mark, known to the Apostle Simon Peter as a young man in Jerusalem who next appears accompanying Paul and Barnabas to Antioch (Acts 12:12, 25). Years later, Mark was in Rome at the same time as Peter (1 Peter 5:13), and it seems he faithfully wrote down the Apostle's oral accounts of the world-changing ministry and sayings of Jesus Christ because much of this Gospel bears the features of eyewitness testimony. Mark was written in Greek and aimed at a Gentile audience. As the shortest of the Gospels and closest in time to the historical Jesus, it is a good one to read as an introduction to the Christian story. The theme throughout is the way the teachings, death, and resurrection of Jesus Christ, the Son of God, introduce a new beginning for humanity with the 'Kingdom of God'. The material is repeated in the Gospels of both Matthew and Luke, and the three together are known as the Synoptic Gospels. In one of Jesus' sayings he urges his followers to listen to his teaching, 'Take heed what ye hear: with what *measure* ye mete, it shall be *measured* to you: and unto you that hear shall more be given. For he that hath, to him shall be given: and he that hath not, from him shall be taken even that which he hath' (4:24–25). These sayings and the events of the Gospel story are carefully organised by Mark, and he frames them between the heavens being torn apart at Jesus' baptism and the Temple curtain being torn in two at his crucifixion (1:10–11, 15:38–39). Thus the life of Jesus, God's 'incarnation', tears away the barriers between heaven and earth, between the Temple sanctuary and the people. A feature of Mark's Gospel is the way the significance of Christ as Messiah is treated as a secret for his followers, as if to guard against Jesus being hailed as an earthbound, political Messiah.

About the Phrase
In terms of its use in other media, the phrase is virtually exclusive to Shakespeare's *Measure for Measure*. In the play, Angelo condemns Claudio to death, but the benign Vincentio tricks him to commit a similar crime and threatens like judgement: 'An Angelo for Claudio, death for death! Haste still pays haste, and leisure answers leisure;

Like doth quit like, and *Measure* still *for Measure*' (Act V, scene 1). At the end of the intrigues, mercy prevails. The prevalence of the phrase in English today probably owes as much to the title of the Shakespeare play as it does to the biblical saying, but both build on the ancient *lex talionis*, the retaliatory law of like being repaid with like (see page 7).

The Gospel according to St Luke

Blind leading the blind
Uninformed and incompetent people leading others who are similarly incapable

Luke, the 'beloved physician' (Colossians 4:14), is a disciple of Paul the Apostle and author of the Acts of the Apostles (see page 68) as well as of this Gospel. He dedicates both to Theophilus, and begins with his claim to have 'investigated the whole course of these events in detail' (1:3, Revised English Bible). He presents Jesus as the Jewish Messiah, but his eagerness to show Greeks and Romans how God is at work in the history he has researched is striking. Luke never knew Jesus; his starting point appears to have been the account of Mark with the Gospel of Matthew contributing supplementary information. His research garnered much additional material: for example, Luke gives extra information on the events leading up to the births of both John the Baptist and Jesus, and on the childhood of Jesus. In one instance he seems to combine separate texts from Matthew into a parable: 'And he spake a parable unto them, Can the *blind lead the blind*? Shall they not both fall into the ditch? The disciple is not above his master: but every one that is perfect shall be as his master. And why beholdest thou the mote that is in thy brother's eye, but perceivest not the beam that is in thine own eye?' (6:39–41; compare to Matthew 7:3, 10:24, and 15:14). Only Luke relates the parable of the 'Prodigal Son' (15.11–32) and the vivid story of an encounter of two disciples with the risen Jesus on the road to Emmaus (24:13–35). A distinctive feature of this Gospel is the humanity of Jesus, his concern for the poor and marginalised, his keen interest in people, the dangers of wealth, the importance of prayer and thanksgiving, and Luke's distancing of Jesus from Israel's political ambitions. A particular feature of Luke's message is the role of God's Holy Spirit in the Gospel story, starting with the enabling of Jesus' birth, the recognition of his significance, and the initiation of his ministry (1:35, 2:25–27, 3:22). Unique to Luke's Gospel is a verse after the *Lord's Prayer* asserting that the gift of God's Holy Spirit is available to inspire the lives of all who sincerely seek it (11:13).

About the Phrase

This metaphor has ancient origins, and Jesus may have been using an existing expression that his hearers would have instantly understood. It even appears in the *Katha Upanishad*, a fourth-century BCE Indian book of teachings, but this is unlikely to have been an influence. The Irish playwright George Farquhar (1678–1707) wrote in *Love and a Bottle* (1698): 'When the *blind lead the blind*, no wonder they both fall into matrimony' (Act V, scene 1). The phrase seldom appears as a title, and in today's world of political correctness its use as a metaphor for incompetence might well invite censorship!

The Gospel according to St John

Cast the first stone
Be quick to blame, criticise, or punish, without considering one's own shortcomings

John's Gospel is distinct in character from, and was written later than, the other three. From the second century onwards, the author was accepted as John, son of Zebedee and one of the twelve disciples, but new research makes a good case for this Gospel being a carefully constructed work by John the Elder of Ephesus (see pages 92 and 95) who might well have been a young man in Jerusalem at the time of the main narrative. Indeed, the author may have been the unnamed one of two disciples of John the Baptist who followed Jesus after his baptism (1:35–40). In the narrative at the end of the Gospel (21:1–23) the identity of the second of two disciples following Jesus is revealed (21:20). The author proceeds to identify himself as this disciple, claiming personal testimony (21:24). At the Last Supper Jesus indicated his betrayer to this same disciple, who may not have been one of the twelve (13:21–27, Mark 14:20), but one for whom Jesus had a special regard (21:20–24) and to whom at his crucifixion he entrusted his mother (19:25–27). In the opening prologue John sets Jesus in a cosmic scope, echoing Genesis (1:1–18). He relates seven miracles as signs that Jesus is the Messiah: three demonstrating his command over nature (2:1–11; 6:5–13; 6:16–25), of which the feeding of the five thousand is the only miracle common to all four gospels; three miraculous healings (4:43–54; 5:1–9; 9:1–14); and the momentous raising of Lazarus (11:1–44). Distinctive features are the indications of eyewitness testimony, the quantity of material unique to this Gospel, the devotion of almost half the book to the events surrounding the crucifixion and its significance, one of Christianity's most important Bible verses (3:16), and the emphasis on love. This final aspect included Jesus' 'New Commandment' for his followers to 'love one another', through which the world would then know that, by their mutual love, they were his own (13:34–35) and believe in him (17:20–21). In the story of the fallen woman (8:1–11), Judaic law demanded stoning, but Jesus challenges her accusers, saying that 'He that is without sin among you, let him *first cast a stone at her*' (8:7). He thus undermines the morality of the punishment and establishes a new basis for justice with forgiveness and reform being preferable to retribution.

About the Phrase
Cast the first stone is frequently used as a title across a wide range of media, including articles in magazines and periodicals, books, and popular music albums. A report on prostitution in the USA by Murtagh and Harris was published under this title in 1957. Stoning survives to this day as a legal form of capital punishment in a number of countries despite the fact that it is considered a form of torture, such that it violates both human rights and international law. Though the fatal stone may be unidentifiable, each person casting a stone carries an inescapable culpability. In this lies the brilliance of Jesus' response and the power of the phrase.

The Acts of the Apostles

Kick against the pricks
Argue and fight against people in authority

The events recorded in this gripping record by Luke, a Greek physician who was an eyewitness for much of the action, follow straight on from his Gospel (see page 64). He charts the birth of the Christian religion (11:26) and its spread from Jerusalem through present day Turkey to Greece and Rome, the centre of the Empire. The central characters are the apostles Peter and Paul. The action starts with Jesus' promise following his resurrection that his disciples will be filled with the Holy Spirit, and the amazing story of how this is fulfilled in Jerusalem with three thousand people being converted following an oration by Peter. After dramatic accounts featuring Peter, the action moves to Saul of Tarsus, an ardent Jew and relentless persecutor of the young Christian faith in Jerusalem. In an extraordinary story, Saul encounters the risen Jesus on the road to Damascus who says, 'I am Jesus whom thou persecutest: it is hard for thee to *kick against the pricks*' (9:5), and he is told to take the Gospel to the Gentiles. In a miraculous turnaround (ch. 9), he becomes a fervent champion of Jesus Christ, known as Paul. As we follow Paul on his missionary journeys around Asia Minor and Greece, we are confronted with an action-packed narrative of miracles, martyrdom, powerful speeches, empowerment by the Holy Spirit of God, persecution, personality clashes, beatings, death threats, prison escapes, and a sharp controversy about circumcision. The account concludes with Paul being dispatched on a ship for trial, a dramatic shipwreck, and his arrival in Rome. Faith in Jesus of Nazareth, the Messiah of a Jewish sect, moves quickly to become a worldwide religion. Abraham's faith in the one God becomes an inheritance for the whole world.

About the Phrase

In ancient farming, poles or 'goads' (as in 'goad someone on') with sharp ends were held behind the oxen drawing ploughs to prevent them stopping or going backwards, thus ensuring they moved on forwards. An obstinate ox would *kick against the pricks* and harm itself. The expression may have been an established metaphor, and its Greek form occurs in *Agamemnon,* a Greek tragedy by Aeschylus (525–456 BCE), at line 1624. This KJV phrase comes from ancient texts in the Syriac rather than Greek tradition, and is omitted in most modern translations. However, in a seven-and-half-thousand word sermon preached on 9 September 1866, using the phrase eighteen times, the great Christian evangelist C. H. Spurgeon (1834–1892) explained how *kicking against the pricks,* both as a metaphor and parable, is typical of Jesus as recorded in the Gospels. Spurgeon used it to persuade his listeners that Paul's encounter was genuine. The sensitivity and brilliance of this appeal to Paul is likewise an appeal to all doubters and opponents of Jesus Christ today. The phrase is now firmly established in the English language, straight from the Bible, and appears in titles of both books and songs.

The Epistle of Paul the Apostle to the Romans

A law unto itself/themselves
People and things behaving unusually or disregarding custom

This letter has been dubbed 'the Gospel according to Paul'. It seems that, before either Peter or Paul had arrived in Rome, belief in Jesus as Messiah had already arisen among some Jewish people in the many synagogues there, including Gentile proselytes to the new faith. The letter may date from around 56 CE when most of Rome's Jewish people had been expelled, and it is addressed primarily to these Gentiles. The thrust of Paul's teaching is that both Jews and Gentiles fall short of God's ideals, and both need the forgiveness and salvation made possible by the death and resurrection of Jesus. He explains that 'when the Gentiles, which have not the law, do by nature the things contained in the law, these, having not the law, are *a law unto themselves*' (2:14).

Paul explains that the Jewish tradition of the law and the prophets pointed to Jesus. Gentiles can also inherit the blessings promised to Abraham (see page 5) and his heirs, but are put right with God ('justified') by grace (see page 96) through faith in Christ, without having to take on the traditions that marked out the Jews as such. If Gentiles had to become Jews in order to become followers of Jesus, that would mean relying on what they themselves did ('works') instead of relying on Christ himself. To affirm that Jesus is 'Lord' (10:9) is to affirm his deity and our allegiance in following him alone, as the one whose resurrection assures our own salvation and ultimate resurrection.

About the Phrase

The phrase appears frequently in newspaper headlines, especially to describe maverick behaviour by influential people such as politicians and football managers. Variations of *a law unto themselves* occur as book titles, but this is one of the few biblical phrases that has not penetrated the world of music. The poet John Milton's (1608–1674) epic work, *Paradise Lost* (1667), despite depicting the conflict between good and evil in terms of powerful Old Testament Hebrew imagery, also reflects the comparatively enlightened world of the New Testament in such lines as:

> God so commanded, and left that command
> Sole daughter of his voice; the rest, we live
> *Law to ourselves,* our reason is our law
>
> ***Paradise Lost, Book 9***

The First Epistle of Paul the Apostle to the Corinthians

All things to all men
The ideal of pleasing everyone even though this is never possible

This letter is one of the very earliest parts of the New Testament. It contains Paul's famous eulogy to love, 'but the greatest of these is charity' (i.e., love; see 13:1–13), a written account of Jesus' Last Supper which may predate the Gospels (11:23–26), and the assertion of an imperishable life after death (15:50–57). Corinth was a busy Greek trading port and Paul had founded the church there in

50–51 CE, but within a few years some among the congregation were behaving in unacceptable ways, failing to understand the new Christian faith and quarrelling. He explains the power that comes from the death and resurrection of Jesus, and sets out a pattern for morals and ethics in the context of those times. In serving as one of Jesus' apostles, Paul explains that he is released from his strict Jewish background and thus becomes free to extend his reach to Gentiles, outcasts, and the poor in ways they each could understand, as it were, becoming *all things to all men* (9:22). Paul devotes a whole chapter to 'spiritual gifts'. He explains that these Christian attributes are for the common good of the community, and cannot be earned or merited as they come freely through God's Holy Spirit, the only source of each Christian's ability truly to accept Jesus as 'Lord' (12.3). The greatest of these gifts is Christian love, as described in chapter 13 of the epistle.

About the Phrase
All things to all men is employed as the title in a wide range of songs, presentations, and writings; sometimes of a salacious or amoral nature, denoting a compromise of principle to reach a wide audience, thus perverting the original usage as found in the Bible. It was chosen by writer/director George Isaac as the title for his debut feature film, a thriller movie, set in London and released in 2013; the piece was later retitled. In today's world of conflicting demands on time and attention, the phrase is most often used in the sense of it being impossible to keep everyone happy and satisfy them all without compromising one's principles. Seen another way, when someone sets aside some of their ingrained prejudices in consideration of another's point of view, the aim encapsulated in being *all things to all people* can become not only possible but a virtue.

The Second Epistle of Paul the Apostle to the Corinthians

A thorn in one's flesh
The cause of a persistent irritation, annoyance, or affliction

Paul wrote this second letter to Christians in Corinth a few years after the first. Ongoing difficulties with their new faith were compounded by the arrival of some arrogant new leaders whom he describes as false apostles (11:13). With a deep sense of pastoral concern and calling, Paul deals with these problems using his own sufferings as examples to correct their shallow, faulty version of Christianity. In doing so he ranges from ecstatic joy to angry depression and lays himself bare, pointing out that the heart of the faith is in Christ's own suffering on the cross. In chapter 6 he appeals for this to be given a central place in their lives, and in chapter 12 counts his own *thorn in the flesh* as something of value as it keeps him aware of his weaknesses, while remaining reliant on God's strength (12:7). chapters 8 and 9 are the most thorough account anywhere in the Bible of the proper motives for charitable Christian giving and make an appeal in support of the beleaguered church in Jerusalem.

About the Phrase
The graphic expression *thorn in the flesh* first occurs in this biblical passage, but the nature of the complaint from which Paul suffered is unknown and has been the subject of much conjecture. The metaphor has its origins in the Old Testament which may give clues to its meaning (e.g., Numbers 33:55 and Joshua 23:13). This vivid idiom is widely used as the title of both religious and secular books. D H Lawrence (1885–1930) wrote a book of short stories in 1913

with the title *Vin Ordinaire*, but this was revised and published in 1914 with its new title, *The Thorn in the Flesh*.

The Epistle of Paul to the Galatians

Fall from grace
A loss of status, respect, or prestige

This, one of Paul's earliest letters, is addressed to churches he had established by winning converts from the heathen population in Galatia, a Roman province in Asia Minor. However, some Jewish leaders had arrived who claimed that, to enjoy the blessings promised to the descendants of Abraham, these Gentiles must be circumcised under the Jewish law. Denouncing this notion, Paul builds up a theological doctrine that justification as God's people rests on faith alone. As an Apostle, he claims divine authority and explains how God's promise to Abraham, that he would be the father of nations (Genesis 17:3–5), preceded the law and depended on his faith. He brands these Judaizers as troublemakers, warning the churches that if they heed their advice they will have *fallen from grace* and from freedom in Christ as saviour (5:4). Paul contrasts the blessings of a life based on God's spirit of love with a destructive lifestyle (5:13–6:2).

About the Phrase
The idiom of a *fall from grace* originates in this Bible passage, but the sense of 'grace and favour' and the corresponding ignominy of disgrace is different from the biblical concept. In its common usage the phrase is popular with headline writers and as a title for books, songs, albums, and films. For Christians, *grace* is the generous, free, and totally undeserved gift from God through which faith is enabled and 'salvation' experienced. A *fall from grace* might consist of putting oneself out of reach of this free gift of God by deliberate sinfulness or a hypocritical striving to win God's favour and be recognised.

The Epistle of Paul the Apostle to the Ephesians

Fullness of time
The right or appropriate time for an event to occur

This letter makes one of the most mature and bold claims in the New Testament for the power of the Christian faith. Paul founded the church in Ephesus, and he may well have written this letter from prison with the years of his ministry behind him (3:1; 6:20). In it he asserts that followers of Christ were part of God's eternal plan, 'That in the dispensation of the *fulness of times* he might gather together in one all things in Christ, both which are in heaven, and which are on earth' (1:10). Ephesus, with its congregation of both Jewish believers and converted Gentiles, was the most fully developed of the first churches. Distinctive features of the letter are the organic nature of a joined-up church, living in unity in the light of Christ, God's free gift of Grace, the power of his Holy Spirit to give wisdom and insight, and the importance of prayer. Distinctive types of ministry are listed (4:11–12), as too are the features of the 'full armour of God' (6:11–18). Both family and community should imitate Christ in unity and in love. The letter ends with practical directions for doing this.

About the Phrase

The phrase *fullness of time* occurs frequently as part of the title in books, films, articles, and music. In Galatians 4:4 (KJV) Paul writes: 'when *the fulness of the time* was come, God sent forth his Son'. In the modern age of quick fixes and demands for immediacy, the patience not to rush into action but to wait for a propitious moment is a virtue well worthwhile.

The Epistle of Paul the Apostle to the Philippians

Book of life

An imaginary book of righteous souls

Philippi was a Roman colony near the north Aegean coast and site of the first church founded by Paul in Europe. Luke gives a gripping account of Paul's time there (see Acts 16:12–40). These Philippians provided continuing financial support to his missionary work, and the female converts played an important role in spreading the new faith. Paul had a special bond with this young church and he urges its congregation to stand firm, even in the face of suffering and conflict. One of the letter's features is its moving Hymn to

Christ (2:5–11), which is among the most profound assertions of the divinity and humanity of Jesus. Paul sees his former Hebrew zeal as worthless, contrasting it with rewards of his new faith in both the power of Christ's resurrection and the righteousness that is God's gift in response to faith. Paul names individuals who have laboured with him and other 'fellowlabourers, whose names are in *the book of life*' (4:3). The letter ends with profuse thanks for the Philippian church's gifts.

About the Phrase

In the New Testament, *book of life* appears first here and seven times again in Revelation. 'May your name be inscribed in the *Book of Life*' is a common Jewish New Year greeting. The Old Testament 'book of the living' is more to do with the 'here and now', belief in life after death being a late concept in Hebrew biblical writings only held by Pharisees (e.g., Daniel 12:1–3 and post-biblical texts). The phrase is a title of books and other media. In the French produced American millennial film, *The Book of Life* (1998), Jesus returns to herald the apocalypse in contemporary Manhattan with Lucifer, Mary Magdalene, and others. This title has also been chosen for a 3D computer-animated fantasy film released by 20th Century Fox in 2014. The pervasive way in which biblical phrases and characters can influence modern media marks the enduring power of the Bible in today's secular culture.

The Epistle of Paul the Apostle to the Colossians

Vain deceit
Empty and misleading argument

Paul never went to Colossae (in European Turkey), but the church there had been founded by one of his fellow workers. His letter begins with greetings and encouragement, first in the supremacy of Christ and then in the mystery of God's salvation revealed in the resurrection. In Greek culture at that time there was much philosophical discussion and heathen worship. It seems young Christian converts were being led astray and beguiled by teachers who had concocted an amalgam of Jewish beliefs with these influences, promising heightened spiritual experience. Paul gets to the point with a strong warning against such false teaching. 'Beware lest any man spoil you through philosophy and *vain deceit*, after the tradition of men, after the rudiments of the world, and not after Christ' (2:8). Later in the letter Paul urges the church to welcome John Mark, cousin of his colleague Barnabas (4:10), showing that a bitter dispute about him with Barnabas had been resolved (Acts 15:36–40).

About the Phrase
In his poem, *The Triumph of Music* (1804), Canto V, William Hayley (1745–1820) wrote:

> Hope! thou sweet, and certain treasure!
> Thou art not a *vain deceit*;
> Thou alone art perfect pleasure;
> Others only charm and cheat.

The phrase mostly occurs in religious discussion, articles, and sermons. As the gulf between modern thought and Bible-based religion widens, with other types of spirituality growing in popularity, this verse with its caution against the *vain deceit* of philosophising receives much attention. In contrast to the uncompromising stance of biblical fundamentalists, modern defenders of Christianity seek to reconcile scientific discoveries, Christianity's revealed truths, and humanity's innate sense of beauty and goodness. The gap between science and religion begins to narrow as scientists find the 'nothing' of emptiness less of a reality and theologians grow in their understanding of the transcendental nature and ultimate unknowability of God. (For Christians, God is revealed as the Trinity of Father, Son, and Holy Spirit, whom they experience in prayer, in worship, and through each individual's life journey of discipleship.)

The First Epistle of Paul the Apostle to the Thessalonians

Labour of love
Work undertaken freely for the pleasure it gives

The Book of Acts recounts the founding, on Paul's second missionary journey, of a church in what is now Salonika on mainland Greece (Acts 17:1–17). It seems Jewish synagogues had sprung up around the Mediterranean, garnering many Gentile proselytes to their monotheistic faith. Paul's converts included many god-fearing Gentiles as well as Jewish believers, but his claims for the Christian

Gospel attracted fierce opposition from a Jewish faction. For his own safety, Paul was sent off to another town, but the mob followed and he was packed off on a ship to Athens. This letter is one of Paul's earliest, written soon after his visit, in which he tells this young church how he thanks God for them in his prayers, remembering their 'work of faith, and *labour of love*, and patience of hope in . . . Christ . . . having received the word in much affliction' (1:3–6). Two particular themes in this letter are the expectation of Christ's second coming and the need for Christians to live holy and sexually moral lives. Paul gives an assurance (4:17) that both the living and those who have died will 'ever be with the Lord'.

About the Phrase
The phrase *labour of love* also occurs at Hebrews 6:10. It has been suggested that the KJV translators, in coining the phrase, may have been influenced by the title of Shakespeare's play, *Love's Labours Lost* (1588), especially as the pre-Shakespearean translations use different phrasing. In common usage, the phrase is often applied to personal efforts that go well beyond basic expectations. The phrase has wide application, ranging from song titles, through manufactured goods, and even to the paraphernalia of childbirth.

The Second Epistle of Paul the Apostle to the Thessalonians

Busybodies/busybody
Meddlesome mischief-makers

This second letter may well be a follow-up to the first, to correct a misunderstanding about the timing of the expected second coming of Jesus. He reassures the young Christians in Thessalonica that they need not be troubled by claims of 'the day of the Lord' being imminent. He explains how at first there will be a manifestation of evil which will be annihilated in the light of Christ's return (2:8–10). In the meantime, he thanks God for choosing them, and urges them to stand firm, taking comfort in God's love and the good hope that is theirs through all they have learned about Jesus (2:13–15). It seems the trouble stems from some self-opinionated hangers-on who have not enough to do. Paul, noting 'there are some which walk among you disorderly, working not at all, but are *busybodies*' (3:11), tells the faithful to disassociate themselves from the troublemakers. These should be admonished as family members, not enemies, and urged to settle down to find gainful employment so that God may give them his peace.

About the Phrase
Its meaning is so different from that of its constituent words that *busybody* is an idiom within itself. The KJV also has the word in 1 Timothy 5:13 and 1 Peter 4:15. Its idiomatic sense may come from the context in these passages. The first known use of the word was in the Tyndale Bible (1525), but in the Coverdale Bible of 1535 the words are split in two as a phrase. In book titles and other media,

the words are often separated and used for topics relating to physical activity, playing on the currency of the idiom.

The First Epistle of Paul the Apostle to Timothy

The root of all evil
Greed, excessive worldly desire

The two letters to Timothy and the one to Titus are known as the *Pastoral Epistles*, dealing as they do with church life and pastoral care. In Acts, Timothy is featured as a close companion of Paul, but these letters are from a later period and differences in style suggest they may have been composed after Paul's death. This letter's purpose is clearly stated at 3:15. Church life had become well developed with bishops and deacons and, it seems, women had become active in church leadership. They are instructed to resume a subordinate place, in keeping with society at that time. In particular, the letter warns against the lure of worldly wealth, 'For the love of money is *the root of all evil*: which while some coveted after, they have erred from the faith, and pierced themselves through with many sorrows' (6:10). They should rather trust in the richness of the living God (6:17–19). The letter is an example of appropriate rules and conduct being set for the prevailing culture of the day. It begs the question about the relevance of these rules when cultures move on and customs change.

About the Phrase

George Bernard Shaw (1856–1950) reckoned the lack of money to be *the root of all evil*, and the Danish philosopher Søren Kierkegaard (1813–1855) wrote that boredom is *the root of all evil*. In his short story, *The Root of all Evil*, Graham Greene (1904–1991) suggests secrecy as the source. But the original Greek text of 1 Timothy says that *philarguria*—'the love of money'—is *the root of all evil*. This puts the blame on misplaced desire rather than on money as such. By omitting 'love', the popular moral saying 'money is *the root of all evil*' is in fact a misquotation of the Bible. In the *Vulgate* (the Latin Bible) *philarguria* is translated as *cupiditas*, meaning lust or strong desire, and the saying had a much wider application. The writer may have quoted a popular saying of his time about the evils of avarice (see Proverbs 15:27 and Matthew 6:19). The phrase appears in a wide range of book and media titles which sometimes misquote the Bible, wrongly defining *the root of all evil* as money.

The Second Epistle of Paul the Apostle to Timothy

Fight the good fight
Keep hold of beliefs/principals without giving in

This letter describes a situation in which the church is under persecution and it appears that Paul was facing martyrdom as a prisoner in Rome around 67 CE, but there are no certain records of this. Timothy was a well-respected Greek believer from Lystra in Asia Minor whom Paul had recruited amid controversy about the need for Gentiles to be circumcised (Acts 15:1–16:3). Paul treated Timothy as his son (1 Corinthians 4:17), naming him as a close colleague in five of his letters, so he was keen to hand on to him the cares and concerns of his own ministry. In this letter we find Timothy grappling with false teachers who are leading the church astray. This letter covers similar ground to the first (see page 82) but with encouragement rather than instructions, with Paul offering his own life as a model in teaching and suffering. Paul gives a list of godless behaviour (3:1–5) and his guidance is for the whole church community. He writes '. . . the time of my departure is at hand. I have *fought a good fight*, I have finished my course, I have kept the faith' (4:6–7).

About the Phrase
Keep fighting the good fight is commonly used today to spur people on in the face of difficulty. *Fight the good fight* (1 Timothy 6:12) was a common exhortation for missionary activity in the nineteenth century, when concepts from Old Testament warfare were often used as metaphors for spiritual advance. *Fight the good fight* comes in the first line of a well known hymn written by John S. B. Monsell and William Boyd in 1863. It is also the title of a moral song in the 1981 *Allied Forces* album of the award winning Canadian hard rock band Triumph, founded in 1975.

The Epistle of Paul to Titus

Filthy lucre
Money from ill-gotten gains

Titus was a co-worker of Paul who had once gone with the Apostle to Jerusalem to see the church leaders there and explain the Gospel they were teaching among the Gentiles (Galatians 2:1–2). Paul relates that he had left Titus on Crete to finish his work (1:4–5), but, as there is no mention of such a visit in Acts, this would have been late in his ministry. This large island with its ancient history was the source of many myths and home of the philosopher Epimenides who, a Cretan himself, made the famous paradoxical claim 'all Cretans are liars'. Against this background, the letter points out the challenges faced by Titus: 'For there are many unruly and vain talkers and deceivers, specially they of the circumcision: Whose mouths must be stopped, who subvert whole houses, teaching things which they ought not, for *filthy lucre*'s sake. One of themselves, even a prophet of their own, said the Cretians are always liars, evil beasts, slow bellies' (1:7, 10–12).

About the Phrase
The derogatory turn of phrase *filthy lucre* also features as a title for books, albums, and pop groups. It was first used in the Tyndale Bible (1525) to denote 'greedy desire for wealth', and was soon applied to the money itself. The phrase is a direct translation of the Greek words *aischros* ('shameful') and *kerdos* ('profit'). Lucre is from the Latin *lucrum* ('profit') which was already associated with avarice in Roman times. The KJV uses the phrase in three other places (1 Timothy 3:3, 8, and 1 Peter 5:2). In the opening chapter of *Thackeray* (1879), Anthony Trollope (1815–1882) comments on

the great novelist's money-making lecture tours: 'When we talk of sordid gain and *filthy lucre*, we are generally hypocrites. If gains be sordid and *lucre filthy*, where is the priest, the lawyer, the doctor, or the man of literature, who does not wish for dirty hands?'

The Epistle of Paul to Philemon

For a season
For a limited but significant period in someone's life or experience

In this poignant letter written from prison, Paul appeals to Philemon at the church in Colossae (in modern Turkey) to receive back Onesimus who had been his slave. It seems Onesimus had stolen from Philemon and run away, theft being a crime punishable by death under Roman law. He had been adopted by Paul while serving him in prison and became a faithful Christian (1:10–17). Paul had explained in his main letter to the Colossians 'there is neither . . . bond nor free: but Christ is all, and in all' (Colossians 3:11). First he commends Philemon as a member of the church and then implores him to accept Onesimus in love as a brother, not just a slave, suggesting they had been separated *for a season* so that he might have him back for good (1:15). In light of the cultural mores of those times, this is a wonderful example of Christian love being put before punitive justice, with restoration replacing retribution. The institution of slavery was subverted by this letter but it was centuries before such teaching took effect.

About the Phrase

This phrase first appears in the Coverdale translation of 1535 where it occurs twice, and then three times in the Geneva Bible of 1587. Shakespeare uses the phrase in *Richard III* (c.1592), Act I, scene 4: 'I trembling waked, and *for a season* after could not believe but that I was in hell'; and in *Cymbeline* (c.1610), Act IV, scene 3: 'The time is troublesome. We'll slip you *for a season*'. In the KJV, the phrase occurs nine times and has been in common use ever since. '*For a Season*' is the name of a Christian rock group in the USA. Lewis Carroll uses the phrase in the second 'Fit' of the *Hunting of the Shark* (Charles Dodgson, 1832–1898):

> The Bellman perceived that their spirits were low,
> And repeated in musical tone
> Some jokes he had kept *for a season* of woe—
> But the crew would do nothing but groan.

The Epistle of Paul the Apostle to the Hebrews

Strangers and pilgrims
Wayfarers, different from those around them

Few today accept the KJV attribution to Paul whose style is quite different. The author wrote in Greek, quoting extensively from the Septuagint version of the Hebrew Scriptures in a style closer to a sermon than a letter, and sets out in densely argued detail the basis for the Hebrew faithful to accept Jesus Christ as the culmination of their own story. Jesus, the same yesterday, today, and tomorrow, is the great high priest whose death on the cross, bearing the sins of all humanity yet without sin himself, secures the hope of being at one with God. The old Law is replaced by the New Covenant, and God will dwell in the hearts and minds of his people. The author lists a range of Old Testament figures that died in the faith of God's promises without actually receiving them, 'but having seen them afar off, and were persuaded of them, and embraced them, and confessed that they were *strangers and pilgrims* on the earth' (11:13; see also 1 Peter 2:11). In the secular world of today, Christians can be seen in a similar light, holding different hopes and values as part of God's eternal purposes.

About the Phrase
Strangers and pilgrims is a popular title for books ranging from novels to serious and theological works, with current listings for over twenty different authors. It also features in music titles and is the name of a band. A collection of short stories by Walter de la Mare (1873–1956), touching on the supernatural or the fantastic, was published under this title in 2007. In *Strangers and Pilgrims Once More* (2014), Addison Hodges Hart (1956–) asks the question:

> After seventeen centuries of safety in Christendom what sort of Church must Christians become in a post-modern world, no longer able to count on society for support of Christian ideals?

The General Epistle of James

The patience of Job
The strength to endure trials, disasters and discouragement without losing faith

The author of this book is traditionally accepted as James, the brother of Jesus, who became the leader of the Christian church in Jerusalem. Although Jesus' ministry lacked backing from his family, he appeared to James after his resurrection (1 Corinthians 15:7). The letter is addressed to the twelve tribes scattered abroad and makes various references to the Hebraic tradition, including this reference to Job. It is thus understood to be addressed to Hebrew believers in Christ rather than to Gentile converts. The core of James' message, referring to *the patience of Job* (5:11), seems to be that good actions and the strength to endure suffering are the natural product of an underlying faith. This underlines the teaching of Jesus, who repeatedly criticised the Scribes and Pharisees for obeying the letter of the Jewish law while failing to observe the basic principles of considerate behaviour. The letter is an important endorsement of a faith lived out from day to day.

About the Phrase
The first recorded appearance of this expression in literature is here in this letter of James. The Old Testament story of Job (see page 29) and his patience in adversity is so well known that the idiom *the patience of Job* has become proverbial and occurs widely both in literature and songs as well as in general conversation. In his essay 'Of Adversity', Sir Francis Bacon (1561–1626) wrote, somewhat cynically, 'the pencil of the Holy Ghost hath laboured more in describing the afflictions of Job, than the felicities of Solomon'.

The First Epistle General of Peter

Multitude of sins
Large number of moral offences

This letter is addressed to scattered Christians, both Jewish and Gentile, who were suffering persecution. Peter urges them to stand firm, pointing out that there is much to be learnt from suffering (1:6–7). As Christ had borne suffering, so their own should not be unexpected (4:12; see also page 58) and was no disgrace, provided it did not result from secular crime (4:15). He links their new status as 'children of God' (1:14–16) with the need for a corresponding high standard of behaviour. Peter urges that love and mutual respect be shown in the way life is lived, particularly between husbands and wives, pointing out that an attitude of love makes up for *a multitude of sins* (4:8; see also James 5:20). He exhorts them to thrive on Christ, 'So come to him, to the living stone which was rejected by men but chosen by God and of great worth to him. You also, as living stones, must be built up into a spiritual temple' (2:4–5, Revised English Bible). 'Peter', the nickname Jesus gave to Simon (Luke 6:14), is derived from the Greek/Latin for 'stone' (*petros/petra*), so these references to stones are convincing evidence that Peter is the author, perhaps with Mark as scribe (see page 63) and Silvanus as messenger (5:12).

About the Phrase
The popular saying derived from this verse (4:8) is 'Love covers *a multitude of sins*'. Its appeal comes from being a ready excuse of conscience and its virtue in enabling non-judgemental comment. The phrase is often used in lyrics and by moralisers, and is the title of a novel by Richard Ford published in 2003. Sir Charles Napier

(1786–1860) is famously quoted as having stated: 'Success is like war and like charity in religion, it covers *a multitude of sins*'.

The Second Epistle General of Peter

Wells without water
Useless or corrupted resources

This letter covers similar ground to the letter of Jude. It contains stern warnings about false teachers who will bring destruction upon themselves, as did the false prophets of the Old Testament. The background seems to be a growing impatience for Christ's return and the allure of these false teachers in the mean-time, towards the sinful pleasures of life and away from the life of righteousness in Christ. Greedy for their own commercial profit, they will gain many adherents, luring new converts back to their former ways and bringing the faith into disrepute. Unlike wells that are the source of precious life-giving water, these imposters are *wells without water* (2:17). Impatience is misplaced since 'one day is with the Lord as a thousand years, and a thousand years as one day' (3:8), and nobody knows when or how Christ will return. Scholars have expressed doubt about the author really being Peter, despite his claim to having been present at the transfiguration (1:18; compare to Mark 9:2–8).

About the Phrase
This expression has been used as the title of both songs and books. *Wells* and the springs that feed them have great significance in civilisation. They have been among the earliest places of human worship, and we talk about the 'wellspring of life', itself a biblical phrase (Proverbs 16:22). Jacob's Well in Nablus, north of Jerusalem, has a religious tradition stretching back well over three thousand years. Holywell is a very common place name in Britain, which also has a city and several places named *Wells*, as does North America. Far from being simply unproductive, *wells without water* are, metaphorically, a denial of the very essence of life. The Bible contains other similar metaphors, such as Jude's 'clouds . . . without water' and 'trees . . . without fruit' (Jude 12), which, though just as descriptive, lack both the alliteration of *wells without water* and the association with the 'water of life' (see also John 4:6–26).

The First, Second, and Third Epistles of John

Love one another
To have a shared, mutual love

The first is a general letter, but the others are to particular addressees. A strong new case has been put forward that these letters, together with Revelation, are from the same author as the Gospel of John, the disciple whom Jesus loved, and that he was not one of 'the twelve', but another who had outlived them to become known as 'The Elder' (see page 66). The letters are written with clear authority, which is now claimed to have the nature of eyewitness testimony (1 John

1:1–4). In the first two letters, the theme is love in the context of truth expressed in Jesus and the Christian community. John gives warm encouragement in the face of the schism and heresy that are emerging in the church, and warns sternly against these, urging his readers to *love one another* with the same love that God showed in sending Jesus Christ (1 John 3:11, 23; 4:7–12; 2 John 1:5). In the third letter, John expresses this particular form of affection in the Christian love that he has for his friend Gaius, and warns about a leader who is turning believers away from the congregation with spiteful accusations, the very opposite of the kind of love Jesus expects to be the characteristic of his followers (3 John 9–11).

About the Phrase

In John's Gospel the phrase *love one another* is recorded as a 'new commandment' from Jesus to his disciples. Everyone would then know by their mutual love that they were his own (John 13:34–35). Jesus later prays for all who have been converted through the words of the disciples, that their mutual love will enable the world to believe that he is sent to them by God (John 17:20–21). Tertullian said of Christians 'See, they say, how they *love one another*' (*Apologeticus*, 39, *c*.200 CE). In this twenty-first century there appears to be growing recognition of the past and present evils of bitter divisions within Christianity. The history of doctrinal and sectarian conflict suggests that real healing is more likely to come from active obedience to this command than through intellectual compromise.

The General Epistle of Jude

The way of Cain
The way of envy and greed that leads to hatred and murder

The author calls himself a 'brother of James'. This was a common name but he could well be a brother of James, the leader of the early church in Jerusalem (see page 89), and thus also a brother of Jesus (Matthew 13:55). The letter is indeed considered to have been written early in the life of the Church. Using strong language and examples from the Old Testament, he condemns false teachers who undermine Jesus' teachings as they 'have gone in *the way of Cain*' (1:11), and lead Christians astray towards sin and destruction. Jude explains 'for profit they have plunged into Balaam's error; they have rebelled like Korah, and they share his fate' (1:11, Revised English Bible; see also KJV: Numbers 22-24 and 16:1-34). Key to this deception is the flawed idea that God's grace permits a life of serial sinning and forgiveness. The story of Cain killing his brother Abel out of jealousy is found in Genesis, ch. 4, but some of the material in this short letter reflects writing that is external to the Bible. Much Christian moralising has been based on the contrast between the ways Cain and Abel sought favour with God (Hebrews 11:4). The ending of the letter has a short hymn of praise used in Christian worship through the centuries; it offers glory to the one and only sovereign and eternal God whose love is the way to eternal life through Jesus Christ (1.21-25).

About the Phrase

The Way of Cain is much used as a title for Christian books and other writings, mainly in North America. One of these, a book by Sandra and Rachel Turner (2006), draws on current events and biblical and historical research, revealing the complexities of the Arab-Israeli conflict and explaining how these problems fuel radical Islamic terrorism in the world today. Jude's *Cain,* Balaam, and Core were three Old Testament characters who each in their own way attempted to usurp the authority of God. Nowadays, Christians tend to believe that God's way really is one of love rather than violence, that warfare and religious conflicts arise out of human weakness, and that, in a developed world, military defence needs to be very strictly controlled.

The Revelation of St John the Divine

The patience of a saint
The ability to endure faithfully through difficulties

This extraordinary book of prophetic utterances, apocalyptic visions, and symbolic imagery completes the Bible. In dealing with the heavens and matters beyond human comprehension, it arouses even more speculation than Daniel (see page 41). Its author, John, writes from Patmos (1:9) and is the subject of conjecture. By tradition, he is John of the twelve disciples, but, if all twelve had died by the time of the author's visions (21:14), he may be John the Elder of Ephesus (see pages 66 and 92); Patmos lies only sixty miles away from Ephesus by sea. Warnings are issued to seven churches

(1:4–3:22), not one of which has survived. The number seven signified completeness (for example, God rested on the seventh day), and it occurs fifty-four times in this book, which itself completes the Bible. Of interest are the 'saints', who are valued for their prayers (5:8, 8:3–4), their faithfulness in following Jesus even to death (14:4), their worship (15:3), and their obedience: 'Here is *the patience of the saints*: here are they that keep the commandments of God, and the faith of Jesus' (14:12). These qualities only become possible by the grace of God which comes through Jesus Christ (22:21; see also pages iv, 70, 74, 76, and 94). Main themes in this book include Christ the Redeemer, the struggle between good and evil, and ultimate triumph in a 'new heaven and a new earth' (21:1). At the end of his Revelation John writes 'Surely I come quickly. Amen. Even so, come, Lord Jesus' (22:20).

About the Phrase
The patience of a saint is a book and song title as well as being a common expression. The phrase comes from this biblical verse but usually takes the form 'enough to try (or test) *the patience of a saint*', and the subjects are seldom the paragons of virtue described in Revelation. A feature of the early Church was a misplaced expectation among some Christians that Jesus Christ would return within the current generation. This was based on a misunderstanding of the words of Jesus reported at the end of John's Gospel which John goes out of his way to correct: 'yet Jesus said not unto him, He shall not die; but, If I will that he tarry till I come, what is that to thee?' (John 21.23), as if to say the timing of Christ's return was none of their business. After two thousand years of the Christian message spreading around the world, being acted upon and being misunderstood, it seems *the patience of a saint* is needed as much today as it was in the early days of the Church.

Glossary

with meanings of terms as used in this book

Alliteration	Words with related initial letters or sounds grouped for effect
Apocalyptic	Unveiling of heavenly mysteries, often connected with the future
Apocrypha	Biblical texts, largely from the era between the two Testaments, and now printed separately from Protestant Bibles
Apostle	One 'sent forth'; used of The Twelve and of prominent missionaries
Aramaic	Semitic language of ancient Syria which gradually replaced Hebrew
Ark of the Covenant	The sacred chest that held the tablets of the Torah
Atonement	'At-one-ment', reconciliation, especially of God and humankind
Canon	Lists of sacred books pertaining to particular groups
Children of Israel	People of tribes descended from Jacob (renamed Israel)
Covenant	A contract entered between parties with mutual responsibilities
CE, BCE	Years of the Common Era (Christian AD), years Before CE (BC)
Epigram	Concise, witty saying, often paradoxical
Expression	Phrase used conventionally with a particular meaning
Gentiles	Peoples of the world who are not Jewish

Grace	God's favour—the generous, free, and totally undeserved gift from God through which faith is enabled and 'salvation' experienced
Heathen	People not of Abrahamic faiths (Judaism, Christianity, or Islam)
Hebrews	Tribes claiming descent from Abraham, Isaac, and Jacob
Idiom	A phrase, the meaning of which is understood in common usage but cannot be predicted from the meanings of the constituent words
Incarnation	The embodiment of God the Son in human flesh as Jesus Christ
Jews/Jewish	People of Hebrew descent or whose faith is Judaism
Judaism	Faith, based on the Hebrew scriptures, in the one and only God
Judaizer	One who coerces others to follow Jewish customs or rites
Judeans	Inhabitants of the Roman province of Judea after the Exile
Messiah	Prophesied deliverer of Jews; Christian Saviour of humankind
Metaphor	Word or phrase applied to an object or action to which it is imaginatively but not literally applicable
Passover	Jewish festival celebrating deliverance from bondage in Egypt
Patriarchs	Founding forefathers; in the Bible, of the Hebrew people

Pentateuch	Greek/Latin name for the first five books of the Bible as a unity
Pharisees	Ancient Jewish sect believing in life after death and rigorous interpretation of scripture (hence righteousness)
Philistines	Non-semitic people opposed to the Hebrews, defeated by David
Phrase	Group of words forming a conceptual unit but not a sentence
Proselyte	A convert from one faith to another, a Gentile convert to Judaism
Protestant	Religious principles established in the 16th Century Reformation of European Christianity
Proverb	Short pithy saying in general use that embodies a commonplace fact of experience; a saying from the Book of Proverbs
Sadducees	Aristocratic Jewish group (controlled Jerusalem Temple in Jesus' time)
Salvation	God's deliverance of his Chosen People from trouble (OT), or from sin and its consequences through Christ's death and resurrection (NT)
Septuagint	Greek translation of the Hebrew scriptures of around 200 BCE
Torah	Hebrew term for the Pentateuch, meaning the will of God as revealed in Mosaic law
Vicarious	Suffered, undergone or done as a substitute for another

Index to idioms and phrases in the King James Bible

Bible references are given for 150 of the many dozens of everyday phrases found in the King James Bible. Page numbers are given in bold for phrases included in this book.

all things to all men . . . . **71**; 1 Corinthians 9:22

apple of one's eye, the . . . . **10**; Deuteronomy 32:10

backsliding . . . . Jeremiah 2:19

bag with holes, a . . . . **54**; Haggai 1:6

baptism of fire . . . . Matthew 3:11

battering ram . . . . Ezekiel 4:2

blind leading the blind . . . . **64**; Matthew 15:14 ; Luke 6:39

book of life . . . . **76**; Philippians 4:3

broken heart . . . . Psalm 34:18

brother: Am I my brother's keeper? . . . . Genesis 4:9

bucket: a drop in a bucket . . . . Isaiah 40:15

burying one's talents . . . . Matthew 25:25

busybodies/busybody . . . . **81**; 2 Thessalonians 3:11

can two walk together, except they be agreed? . . . . **46**; Amos 3:3

cast pearls before swine . . . . **61**; Matthew 7:6

cast the first stone . . . . **66**; John 8:7

counting the cost . . . . Luke 14:28

daily bread . . . . Matthew 6:11; Luke 11:3

die, better to die than to live . . . . **48**; Jonah 4:3

do as you would be done by . . . . **47**; Obadiah 1:15; Matthew 7:12; Luke 6:31

eat drink and be merry . . . . Ecclesiastes 8:15; Luke 12:19

ends of the earth, the . . . . **56**; Psalm 48:10 ; Zechariah 9:10

eye for an eye, an . . . . **6**; Exodus 21:24; Matthew 5:38

eye: in the twinkling of an eye . . . . 1 Corinthians 15:52

faith to move mountains . . . . Matthew 17:20

fall from grace . . . . **74**; Galatians 5:4

fall on one's sword	22; 1 Samuel 31:4; 1 Chronicles 10:4
fat of the land	Genesis 45:18
feet of clay	Daniel 2:33
fight the good fight	**83**; 2 Timothy 4:7
figs from thistles	Matthew 7:16
filthy lucre	**85**; Titus 1:7
fire and brimstone	Genesis 19:24; Luke 17:29
flesh and blood	Matthew 16:17; 1 Corinthians 15:50
fly in the ointment	33; Ecclesiastes 10:1
fruit: forbidden	Genesis 3:3
fruits, by their fruits ye shall know them	Matthew 7:16
fullness of time	**75**; Galatians 4:4; Ephesians 1:10
gird up one's loins	1 Kings 18:46
give up the ghost	**38**; Lamentations 1:19
give: better to give than to receive	Acts 20:35
glass: see through a glass darkly	1 Corinthians 13:12
gnashing of teeth	Matthew 8:12; Luke 13:28
go the extra mile	Matthew 5:41
God of heaven and earth	**24**; Ezra 5:11
God save the king	**23**; 1 Samuel 10:24; 2 Chronicles 23:11
harden one's heart	Exodus 4:21; Mark 6:52; John 12:40
haves and have nots	Matthew 13:12
heart: a broken heart	Psalm 34:18
heart's desire	Psalm 10:3
honey, sweeter than/sweet as	Judges 14:18; Revelation 10:9
house: set/put one's house in order	**20**; 2 Kings 20:1
inestimable treasure	**1**
kick against the pricks	**68**; Acts 9:5
kill the fatted calf	Luke 15:27
labour of love	**79**; 1 Thessalonians 1:3
labourer worthy of his hire	Luke 10:7

land of Nod, the . . . . 5; Genesis 4:16
laugh to scorn . . . . 26; 2 Kings 19:21; Matthew 9:24, Mark 5:40; Luke 8:53
law unto itself/themselves, a . . . . 70; Romans 2:14
left hand not knowing what the right is doing . . . . Matthew 6:3
leopard: a leopard cannot change its spots . . . . 37; Jeremiah 13:23
lilies of the field . . . . Matthew 6:28
lily among thorns . . . . 34; Song of Songs 2:2
lion's mouth, out of the . . . . 2 Timothy 4:17
live by the sword die by the sword . . . . Matthew 26:52
locust years . . . . 44; Joel 2:25
lost sheep . . . . Matthew 10:6
love one another . . . . 92; John 13:34; 1 John 3:11; 2 John 1:5
love your enemies . . . . Matthew 5:44; Luke 6:27
man after one's own heart, a . . . . 16; Exodus 4:15; 1 Samuel 13:14
many called but few chosen . . . . Matthew 22:14
measure for measure . . . . 62; Matthew 7:2; Mark 4:24; Luke 6:38
mercies, tender mercy . . . . Psalm 25:6; Luke 1:78
mouth of babes and sucklings, out of the . . . . Psalm 8:2; Matthew 21:16
multitude of sins . . . . 90; James 5:20; 1 Peter 4:8
old wives' tales/fables . . . . 1 Timothy 4:7
patience of a saint, the . . . . 95; Revelation 13:10, 14:12
patience of Job, the . . . . 88; James 5:11
peace offering . . . . 9; Exodus 20:24; Numbers 7:88
pearl of great price . . . . Matthew 13:46
physician heal thyself . . . . Luke 4:23
ploughed with my heifer . . . . 13; Judges 14:18
powers: the powers that be . . . . Romans 13:1
pride goes before a fall . . . . 31; Proverbs 16:18
prophet without honour in own country . . . Matthew 13:57; Mark 6:4; John 4:44
put to shame . . . . 53; Psalm 35:4; Zephaniah 3:19
put words in someone's mouth . . . . 18; Exodus 4:15; 2 Samuel 14:3